ITALIAN
COOKING

ITALIAN
COOKING

John Varnom

NEW
BURLINGTON
BOOKS

DEDICATION

Questo libro è dedicato alla Signora Olga Bernardi di
Capanna Kind a Sportinia, senza la quale non avrei potuto
scrivere una sola parola. Ti ringrazio, Olga.

Ringrazio, anche il mio fratello Raisa Giorgio, cuoco
straordinario, Salvatore, campione di scacchi, e tutti i
personali di Capanna Kind: Olgina, Michele, Italo, Claudia,
Pipo, Franco Allemand e Bruno Capelli.

Thanks also to Daphne Page and Kevin Rourke for their
friendship and guidance, and Deirdre Slevin for her good
humor.

Und endlich Helga Röhrs, mein echter Schatz, für alles.

A QUINTET BOOK

Published by New Burlington Books
6 Blundell Street
London, N7 9BH

ISBN 1-86155-364-1

This book was designed and produced by
Quintet Publishing Limited
6 Blundell Street
London N7 9BH

Art Director: Peter Bridgewater
Designers: Ian Hunt, Martin Vincent
Editors: Shaun Barrington, Caroline Beattie
Susie Ward
Photographer: Trevor Wood
Food Preparation and Styling:
Jonathan Higgings, Judith Kelsey

Typeset in Great Britain by
Central Southern Typesetters, Eastbourne
Manufactured in Hong Kong by
Regent Publishing Services
Printed in Singapore by
Star Standard Industries (Pte) Ltd.

Contents

Introduction

First, let me state what is obvious to anyone with a well-balanced personality, flawless taste and a proper experience of Italian knife and fork work: Italian food is better than French. We can support this proposition with a quote if we have to: 'The Chinese taught the Italians to cook and the Italians taught the French.' That this old saying is also a near-granite foundation stone in the dizzy edifice of gastronomic cliché need not trouble us. It happens to be true, for does not history relate how Marco Polo brought noodles and a few other things back to Venice from China and how some time later Catherine de Medici sent her chefs to the court of the Sun King to cook supper for that gang?

However you, in your polite liberal way, may feel it is invidious to rank national cuisines in this manner. In that case, the next time you find yourself strolling an Icelandic beach, tread carefully, or you might fall into their national dish. That confection entails the burying of a superbly fresh whole cod in the sand, until flesh bones and innards run together in a kind of viscous ooze. Preparation time three months, oven temperature anything below zero. Participants at the feast then despatch their portions as quickly as possible with the aid of firewater, concerning which each man agrees to drink at least twice as much as he can hold. The dessert menu is unclear, although it is probably something palate-cleansing involving lichen and raw glacier.

Still undecided? Then try eating, in turn, at each of the first ten restaurants, pubs or cafés you encounter on any drive through any part of the English countryside. Suddenly, the frigid seas of Iceland, its rocky shores, the gun-metal gleam of its ancient ice-fields may seem strangely welcoming.

Back to Italy, however, truly a paradise on earth for anyone but an Italian filling in a ricevuta fiscale or trying to organize the paperwork for a divorce. Why is Italian food so magnificent? And what is a trattoria?

The trattoria — pronounced, by the way, like 'mamma mia' with the stress on the final 'i' — is more or less the Italian equivalent of a bistro. Trattorie are supposed to be simple places and the clearest sign that you are in one will be the absence of a menu. They are also, strictly speaking, family run.

Left Amalfi, the first Italian maritime republic, has a history stretching back to the 6th century AD. It is famous for its fish restaurants and delicacies.

Left Capri, the island in the Bay of Naples where the Emperor Tiberius held his notorious orgies and the Bay of Naples itself, seen from above Sorrento (**right**). Naples, famous for its pizza, is the gastronomic capital of the south.

Of course, strict speaking is scarcely anything to rely on in these anarchic times. Have we not all visited 'trattorie' as big as Mussolini's railway stations, swarming with men in monkey suits brandishing gold-tasselled menus, in which twenty ways of sacrificing veal are lovingly desecribed? In such cases, 'trattoria' is simply thought to be a friendlier way of saying 'ristorante'.

In real-life trattorie, the dishes of the day – a soup maybe, a couple of pastas probably, and three or four main courses – will be described to you in person by whoever takes your order. A wine list would be unusual. And as for those things they shove round on wheels, groaning with out-of-season strawberries, half-a-dozen cash-and-carry gateaux and oranges in caramel, forget it.

In short, a true trattoria will not attempt to offer its customers an extended, pre-set menu or list of wines. On offer will be what the chef has decided to cook that day, and there is no guarantee that his or her ideas will conform to the titles found in cookery books. But what can you expect, apart from spaghetti bolognese?

Perhaps not even that. Bologna, the city from which the sauce takes its name, is the culinary capital of all that is rich in Italian cooking and even the Bolognese think almost twice before serving meat with pasta. Spaghetti bolognese, and the twenty kinds of veal, are items found well-nigh exclusively outside Italy.

From a technical point of view, there is something else found exclusively outside Italy and its astonishing rarity on home territory gives us a big clue to the true nature of the Italian kitchen. This item is sauces in general. The Italians do make besciamella. And there are a thousand sughi for the extraordinary range of pasta available. But there are no sauces in the French sense.

The Italians consider the real basics are the ingredients themselves. Each will have its own merit. The task of the chef is to identify that merit and then tease it out by sympathetic treatment. This frequently means that the actual cooking process is an excessively simple one and, in that respect, I think this book may surprise you a little. The cooking is very much the final touch. Artfully concealed by the dish's very simplicity is the intricate and delicate process by which the combination of ingredients is chosen and its proportions agreed upon. This happens long before work in the kitchen begins. The watchwords are quality and freshness, neither of which need have anything whatever to do with expense.

The one exception to what seems to be a genuine rule of simplicity appears to be pasta. In fact, what the Italians have done here is very clever. Whereas many cuisines serve some form of carbohydrate with the main dish as a kind of bulking agent, the Italians have removed it and elevated it to a course in its own right. This is the role of

risotto, pasta or polenta as starters, their proper place in the Italian scheme of things.

Potatoes, for example, are made into gnocchi and served smothered in Gorgonzola at the beginning. Or the rice is cooked with the ink and the flesh of inkfish and served in a perfumed and glistening black mound. Noodles come with fresh basil and pine nuts, or white truffles, or ceps, or are thinned into spaghetti and served with clams, or garlic and chilli, or tomato and oregano. Once again, the Italians have separated out what other cultures seek to mingle and dealt with each item in a manner appropriate to itself. The flavours are left intact and the portions kept small.

Two things distinguish this separation process. One is the flawless taste we mentioned earlier. The other is Italy's own abundance of miraculous things to eat, an abundance not common to many other countries. But this need not deter anyone: to cook the food in this book, you have only to do some proper shopping.

So skim through the recipes and then set out for the best market, or supermarket, you know. Buy the freshest ingredients you can afford. Then go home and be kind to them, according to the instructions.

Top Outside Florence in the evening, the time of day all Florentines settle down to their evening meal. Florentines eat well but simply, disdaining the complicated sauces and seasonings of other regions. **Right** The harbour at Sorrento, where fish fresh from the sea is the local speciality.

Basic Recipes

Finely Chopped Vegetables for Roasting

TRITTO

This is a pungent, well-seasoned mixture of vegetables preserved in olive oil, which absorbs the tastes of the ingredients and then permeates and lubricates the meat. Kept sealed and reasonably cool, it will keep indefinitely.

How much you make at any time will really depend on the size of your storage jar, which should be of the spring-loaded storage type or have a screw top. My advice is to make as much as possible: you will soon find yourself using it for roasts of all descriptions and not just Italian ones.

Ample instruction is given in the recipes on the use of *tritto* but the general principal is this: any time you roast or pot-roast meat – and sometimes even fish – spread the *tritto* over and around joint. What the tiny, herb-steeped and caramelized vegetables do to the pan juices is amazing.

The ingredients listed show only proportions, by the way. You could start with 20 onions (followed by 20 carrots) if you wished.

INGREDIENTS
1 medium onion
1 carrot
1 clove garlic
½ stick celery
1 bay leaf
1 spring rosemary
6 fresh sage leaves
Enough olive oil to cover when the ingredients are packed

PREPARATION

■ *Very finely dice all the ingredients into 2.5mm/⅛in dice (or use a food grinder or processor). Sift the pieces together so they are thoroughly mixed.*
■ *Cover with olive oil. Try not to use for at least 12 hours. (The* tritto *should be packed quite tightly.)*

Mayonnaise
MAIONESE

MAKES 1¼ CUPS/ 250 ML/½ PT
Preparation time 10 minutes
INGREDIENTS
2 egg yolks
Juice of half a lemon
1¼ cups/300 ml/½ pt olive oil
Salt and freshly ground black pepper to taste

PREPARATION

■ *Vigorously beat the egg yolks with the lemon juice.*
■ *Begin to introduce the oil in the thinnest stream you can manage. Beat constantly as you do so. (You will see the oil 'disappear' into the eggs. It will do so more and more readily as you proceed. Increase the oil flow proportionately.) Season to taste.*

CHEF'S TIPS

The process here is a chemical one known as 'emulsification', in which individual molecules of one liquid are held in suspension by another, in this case the oil and egg yolks respectively.
Simply:
■ Work with ingredients at room temperature, never straight from the fridge.
■ Do not exceed the 2 yolks to 1¼ cups/250 ml/½ pt oil relationship. This is all the oil the eggs can 'hold'.
■ Go slowly with the oil until you're used to the process. The eggs need a little coaxing to start with.

Béchamel Sauce

BESCIAMELLA

MAKES 2 CUPS/ 450ML/¾ PT
Preparation time 15 minutes
INGREDIENTS
2 cups/450 ml/¾ pt milk
60 ml/4 tbsp butter
good ½ cup/50 g/2 oz plain (all-purpose) flour
Salt to taste
Pinch of nutmeg (optional but usual in the Italian version)

PREPARATION

▪ Heat the milk until it is almost boiling. Whilst the milk is warming, melt the butter over a low heat and stir in the flour.
▪ Cook the roux gently for 2–3 minutes over a very low flame. The mixture should not colour.
▪ Dribble the milk gently into the roux, stirring as you go. When all the milk is added, bring the liquid to the boil. Keep stirring.
▪ When the liquid boils, turn down the heat and simmer. Cook for 5 minutes or so. Add salt and nutmeg to taste.

Lumps. There is little to fear in this department. If you have proceeded at the prescribed steady pace, there should be none. If there are, either force the sauce through a sieve (strainer) or liquidize it. Or ignore them altogether: they will cook out later when the sauce is heated for a second time in the dish you intend it for.

Battening Meat Italian Style

This a splendid trick. The toughest meat is rendered tender and the least promising cut can be elevated and extended. It's a great favourite with us restaurateurs. (A word which has no 'n' in it, by the way).

PREPARATION

▪ Take the piece of meat to be battened. Needless to say, it should be boneless.
▪ Place it on top of a sheet of cling-film (plastic wrap) on a reasonably sturdy worktop. Place another piece of film on top.
▪ Working from one side of the meat to the other, set about it with the handiest blunt instrument. A rolling pin will do, although you can buy fancy, flattened battening devices specifically for the purpose. (You must use cling-film [plastic wrap]. Without it, the meat cannot slide and spread easily.)
   The two recipes involving the technique in this book are Veal Escalope with Lemon and Parsley and Rolled and Pot-Roasted Hare. But just think what else you can do:
▪ Bone a chicken leg and batten it flat. You will have a very large chicken escalope that can be cooked in seconds, either breadcrumbed or sautéed with whatever you fancy.
▪ Involtini. Escalopes of meat or fish which have been stuffed with a little something, rolled, pinned in position and then poached or fried. You must be a little delicate when you batten fish, however.
▪ Portions you might never have considered. The two legs and breasts from one chicken will make 8 very substantial-looking Milanese-style escalopes when breadcrumbed.
   This may give you one or two ideas, which is really what cooking is all about. But for rather more specific suggestions, read on.

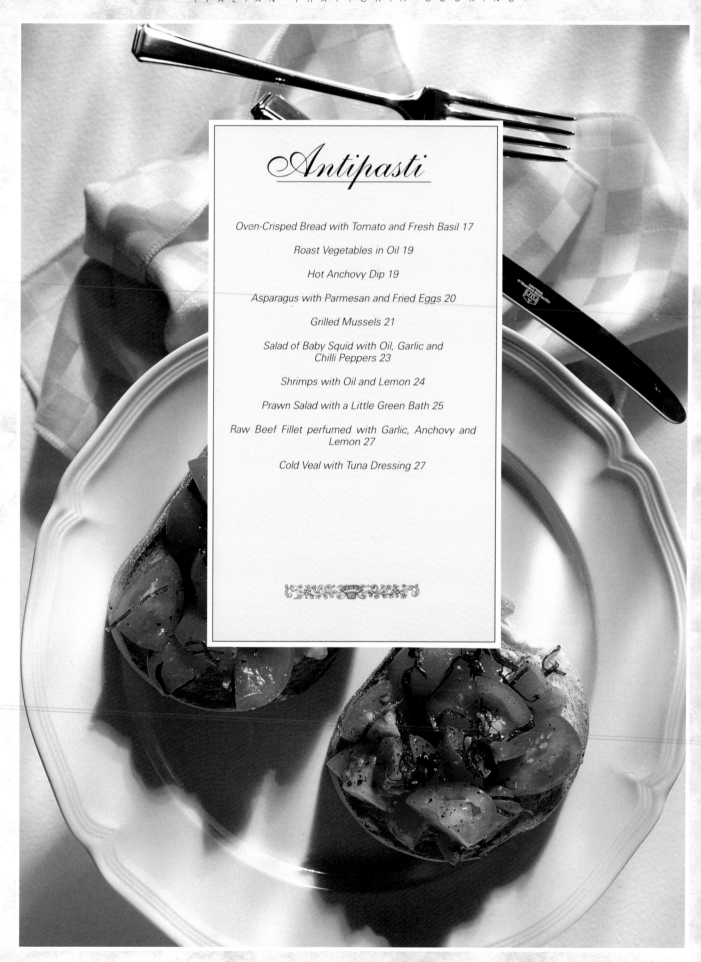

Antipasti

Oven-Crisped Bread with Tomato and Fresh Basil 17

Roast Vegetables in Oil 19

Hot Anchovy Dip 19

Asparagus with Parmesan and Fried Eggs 20

Grilled Mussels 21

Salad of Baby Squid with Oil, Garlic and
Chilli Peppers 23

Shrimps with Oil and Lemon 24

Prawn Salad with a Little Green Bath 25

Raw Beef Fillet perfumed with Garlic, Anchovy and
Lemon 27

Cold Veal with Tuna Dressing 27

Oven-Crisped Bread with Tomato and Fresh Basil

LA BRUSCHETTA

SERVES 6

Preparation time 10 minutes

INGREDIENTS

6 slices thickly-cut white bread, preferably Italian

450 g/1 lb fresh tomatoes

½ cup/50 g/2 oz *fresh* basil

⅔ cup/150 ml/¼ pt olive oil

Salt and freshly ground black pepper to taste

PREPARATION

■ *In a low oven, toast the bread until each slice is completely dry and crisp.*
■ *Roughly dice the tomatoes (there is no need to peel them), and finely chop the basil.*
■ *Add the basil, olive oil and seasoning to the tomatoes.*
■ *Spoon on top of the bread slices and serve immediately. (The bread should still be slightly warm.)*

CHEF'S TIPS

Think this dish is simple? You are right. As you will learn from this book, Italian cooking attains its elegance through simplicity and not complexity. The ideas work so well because of the basic excellence of the ingredients. That is why the basil *must* be fresh. So either make the dish in season or look for an enterprising supermarket. You may also add a clove of crushed garlic at the mixing stage.

Roast Vegetables in Oil

CONTORNI ARROSTI SOTT'OLIO

For an antipasto, allow ½ a sweet pepper, ¼ of a medium aubergine (eggplant) and one courgette (zucchini) per person.

Cooking time 15 minutes

Oven temperature: 190° C/37° F/Gas 5

INGREDIENTS

1 yellow, red or green pepper per 2 people

1 aubergine (eggplant) per 4 people

1 courgette (zucchini) each

⅔ cup/150 ml/¼ pt olive oil per 4 people

Salt and freshly ground black pepper to taste

PREPARATION

■ *Preheat the oven. Halve the peppers and de-seed them. Cut off the coarse stem of the aubergine (eggplant) and trim the courgettes (zucchini).*
■ *Lay the peppers and aubergine (eggplant) directly onto the oven shelves. Do not baste them. Cook for 10 minutes, then add the courgette (zucchini).*
■ *Remove all the vegetables after 15 minutes cooking, when they will be soft.*
■ *Now slice the peppers and aubergines (eggplants) as you will. Simply cut the courgette (zucchini) in half lengthways.*
■ *While everything is still hot, brush with the oil and season to taste.*
■ *Pour over what remains of the oil and serve hot, cold or at room temperature.*

CHEF'S TIP

The vegetables steam in their own juices and thus intensify their own natural goodness. *Basta!*

Hot Anchovy Dip

BAGNA CAUDA

SERVES 6

Preparation time 5 minutes

INGREDIENTS

⅔ cup/150 ml/¼ pt olive oil

45 ml/3 tbsp butter

2 cloves garlic, finely chopped

8 anchovy fillets, finely chopped

PREPARATION

■ *Heat the oil and butter together until the butter melts. As soon as the butter begins to foam, add the garlic.*
■ *After 15 seconds or so, add the anchovy fillets and turn the heat down very low.*
■ *Remove the pan from the heat as soon as the fish has disintegrated. Serve warm.*

CHEF'S TIPS

Bagna Cauda is a dip for raw vegetables. Slice whatever you fancy into batons or florets and simply eat 'em up.

Asparagus with Parmesan and Fried Eggs

ASPARAGI ALLA PARMIGIANA CON UOVE FRITTE

Preparation time 18–20 minutes
Oven temperature 190° C/ 375°F/gas 5
INGREDIENTS
1 kg/2 lb fresh asparagus
Salt to taste
90 ml/6 tbsp butter
½ cup/50 g/2 oz freshly-grated Parmesan cheese
30 ml/2 tbsp olive oil
4 eggs

■ *Preheat the oven. Trim the coarse whitish ends from the asparagus spears.*

■ *Boil the asparagus in salted water for about 10 minutes. (If you can keep the heads above the surface of the water, so much the better. Steamed, they have a better chance of remaining intact.)*

■ *Grease the bottom of a flat, oven-proof dish with one-third of the butter. It should be large enough to accommodate the asparagus in two layers only.*

■ *When the asparagus has cooked, arrange it in the dish.*

■ *Sprinkle the Parmesan over the asparagus and dot it with the remaining butter then bake until the cheese and butter form a light brown crust – about 10 minutes.*

■ *In the meantime, fry the eggs carefully. You must not break the yolks.*

■ *To serve, divide the asparagus into four portions on heated plates. Slide a fried egg over each portion. The crusty, cheesy asparagus is dipped in the egg yolks and eaten by hand with precious little finesse.*

Grilled Mussels
COZZE ALLA GRIGLIA

Preparation time 20 minutes, excluding scrubbing

Oven temperature (If your grill/broiler is small): 200° C/ 400° F/Gas 6

INGREDIENTS

1 kg/2 lb fresh mussels

100 g/4 oz/¼ lb fresh breadcrumbs

½ cup/50 g/2 oz freshly-grated Parmesan cheese

60 ml/4 tbsp finely chopped parsley

4 large cloves garlic, finely chopped

Salt and pepper to taste

⅔ cup/150 ml/¼ pt olive oil

PREPARATION

■ Preheat the oven. Thoroughly scrub the mussels, removing all beards and barnacles.
■ Place a pan of water large enough to hold them all on a low heat, add the mussels and cover. Cook for about 5 minutes.
■ In the meantime, combine the breadcrumbs, Parmesan, parsley, garlic, salt and pepper in a bowl.
■ Take the mussels off the heat, drain, and set aside the liquor.
■ Remove the top shell from each mussel, leaving the flesh ensconced in the lower shell. Discard any mussels which have failed to open. Lay the half-shell mussels on a baking tray and sprinkle the breadcrumb mixture into each shell.
■ Combine the oil and the reserved mussel liquor and pour a little onto each mussel. Return stuffed mussels to a hot grill (broiler), or the preheated oven, and bake for 3-4 minutes.

Salad of Baby Squid with Oil, Garlic and Chilli Peppers

INSALATA DI CALAMARETTI CON AGLIO, OLIO E PEPERONCINI

SERVES 4 — 6
Preparation time 20 minutes

INGREDIENTS
1 kg/2 lb baby squid
Juice of 1 lemon
1 ¼ cups/300 ml/½ pt olive oil
6 medium cloves garlic, sliced *not* crushed
3 green chilli peppers, sliced and de-seeded
Salt and freshly ground black pepper to taste

PREPARATION

■ *Clean the squid (see Cleaning Squid) and slice the bodies into rings.*

■ *Bring at least 4 times the volume of water as you have squid to a brisk boil. Add the lemon juice.*

■ *Plunge the prepared squid into the boiling water and cook until the flesh loses it translucency. This will take no longer than 1 minute. Immediately remove the squid from the pan and plunge it into cold water to stop the cooking process. (see Chef's Tips)*

■ *In a separate saucepan, heat the olive oil until one piece of garlic sizzles fiercely when dropped in. Add all the garlic. Cook at a high heat for 30 seconds or so, then remove from the heat. The garlic will continue to cook.*

■ *When the garlic pieces have turned mid-brown, add the sliced chilli and return the pan to the heat for a further 30 seconds.*

■ *Remove the pan from the heat and allow the cooking to continue. Both garlic and chilli should now be dark brown and patently crunchy.*

■ *Allow the oil, garlic and chilli to cool before you dress the seasoned squid with it.*

CHEF'S TIPS

There are all sorts of subtleties here, and even some cultural stuff into the bargain. But first the subtleties.

Use a large volume of water so that the heat given off, as well as its temperature, remains high. (In physics, heat = mass x temperature. This is why sparks don't burn – although their temperature is high, their mass, and therefore their heat is relatively low.)

The heat is essential since we wish to cook the squid very quickly, one of the only two ways there are of cooking it. The other way is slowly. Anything in the middle makes it rubbery. Lemon juice is added to whiten the flesh. Do this with any poached fish, if whiteness takes your fancy.

Now for the culture. *Aglio, olio e peperoncini* is an Abruzzese sauce often served with pasta. Abruzzi is a province halfway down the Adriatic coast of Italy, between Ancona and Pescara. The provincial capital is L'Aquila. They use chillies in many dishes. Surprising how hot and spicy Italian food can be, isn't it?

Shrimps with Oil and Lemon

GAMBERETTI ALL'OLIO E LIMONE

SERVES 4
Preparation time 10 minutes,

INGREDIENTS
450 g/1 lb smallest fresh shrimps
½ globe fresh fennel; roughly chopped
25 g/1 oz fresh parsely
Juisce of 2 lemons
⅔ cup/150 ml/¼ pt olive oil
Freshly ground black pepper to taste

PREPARATION

■ *Bring 4 times as much water by volume as you have shrimps to a rapid boil. (see Salad of Baby Squid and the relevant Chef's Tips)*

■ *Add the fennel and the parsley and cook on for 3–4 minutes.*

■ *Drop in the shrimps and cook hard for a further 2 minutes, then drain. Discard the water and the vegetables.*

■ *Mix the lemon juice and olive oil. Use this to baste the peeled shrimps.*

■ *Serve, still warmish if you can, generously sprinkled with the pepper.*

Prawn Salad with a Little Green Bath

INSALATA DI GAMBERONI AL BAGNETTO VERDE

SERVES 4

Preparation time 15 minutes

INGREDIENTS

2 very large uncooked prawns (shrimps)

Juice of 1 lemon

1¼ cup/300 ml/½ pt olive oil

60 ml/2 tbsp fresh parsley

¼ cup/25 g/1 oz pine kernels

4 large cloves garlic

6 anchovy fillets

4 capers

PREPARATION

■ Peel the prawns (shrimps) and remove the dark, thread-line intestine if you can find it. (This is not essential.) Either discard the shells or set them aside to make soup or stock with later. (see Zuppa di Pesce.)

■ Bring a copious quantity of water to the boil – at least 4 times the volume of the prawns (shrimps). (see Chef's Tips in Salad of Baby Squid.)

■ Add the lemon juice and poach the prawns (shrimps) for 3–5 minutes.

■ Remove the prawns (shrimps) from the liquid and slice them in half lengthways.

■ There are two ways of making the little green bath. Either put the oil, parsley, pine kernels, garlic, anchovies and capers in a liquidizer and blend until smooth. Or very finely chop parsley, garlic, anchovies and capers; crush the pine kernels, and briskly stir everything into the oil. (In the case of the latter method, let the mixture stand for 10 minutes or so to enable the flavours to mingle well.)

■ Serve the prawns with the sauce as a dip.

CHEF'S ASIDE

The *bagnetto verde* is sharper and more piquant than *pesto* (*see* Noodles with Basil, Pine Nuts and Parmesan Cheese), which it resembles strongly in method of preparation and appearance. It is stunning. I have a Hungarian friend whose grasp of English is particularly suited to confections like this one. According to him, it would knock you off your socks.

Raw Beef Fillet Perfumed with Garlic, Anchovy and Lemon

MANZO CRUDO ALLA ZINGARA

SERVES 4

Preparation time 20 minutes

Marinading time 12 hours

INGREDIENTS

1¼ cups/ 300 ml/½ pt olive oil

4 large cloves garlic

4 anchovy fillets

2 whole chilli peppers

450 g/½ lb fillet steak

Salt and freshly ground black pepper to taste

juice of 2 lemons

PREPARATION

■ Heat the oil over a low heat until it is hot, but not hot enough to fry.
■ Add the garlic, anchovy fillets and the chilli peppers and let them stew in the oil for 20 minutes. (On no account should there be any sizzle. We are not frying these ingredients but letting their flavours soak out into the oil.)
■ While the marinade is cooking, slice the beef as finely as you can. There is no such thing as too fine. Lay the slices out on a flat dish, lightly salt them, add pepper to taste and pour over the lemon juice.
■ Remove the oil from the heat after 20 minutes. Allow it to cool then pour it over the beef.
■ Chill the dish for 12 hours. Before serving, remove the garlic and any intact pieces of anchovy. The chillies can be left.

CHEF'S ASIDE

This dish requires a very sharp knife. It is best eaten with unbuttered, very fresh Italian bread, with which you can also mop up the juices.

Cold Veal with Tuna Dressing

VITELLO TONNATO

SERVES 6

Preparation time 20 minutes

INGREDIENTS

675 g/1½ lb roast veal (see Roast Veal)

⅔ cup/150 ml/¼ pt mayonnaise (see mayonnaise)

75 g/3 oz tuna, canned fresh

⅔ cup/150 ml/¼ pt olive oil

3 anchovy fillets

4 capers

2 tablespoons lemon juice

Freshly ground black pepper to taste

PREPARATION

■ Finely slice the roast veal. (It must be cold.)
■ Make the mayonnaise.
■ Either pour the olive oil into a blender and add all the other ingredients except the pepper, veal and mayonnaise, and blend to a smooth paste, or thoroughly pound the tuna, anchovies and capers. Add the lemon juice and whisk the mixture into the olive oil.
■ Fold the oil and fish mixture into the mayonnaise.
■ Line the base of a flat dish with a thin coating of the mayonnaise mixture. Top it with a series of veal slices. Dress the veal with more of the mixture and continue until you run out of ingredients.
■ Chill for 2–3 hours before serving. Liberally season this dish with black pepper on its final journey to the table.

CHEF'S ASIDE

Italian cooking is full of historic echoes. The fish and meat combination is one of them. Roman cooking used one particular flavouring very extensively. It was called *garum* and it was, by all accounts, a kind of rotted-down fish paste. Almost every savoury dish featured it somewhere, and there were no qualms whatever about intermingling the sea and the land.
Vitello Tonnato, an eerie-sounding combination, demonstrates it perfectly. The dish, suitably relevéed, even appears in France as veal with crayfish sauce. The anchovy, incidentally, is almost certainly *garum's* modern equivalent.

Pasta and Gnocchi

Pasta

SERVES 1

Cooking time about 15 minutes

INGREDIENTS

100 g/¼ lb dried pasta – *past' asciutta* in Italian

Salt to taste

A little olive oil

PREPARATION

■ *Use plenty of water when you cook pasta: 1 1/2 pt water for every 100 g/4 oz pasta. Add about 1.75 ml/¼ tablespoon of salt per litre/2 pints.*
■ *Drop all the pasta in at once and add a little olive oil to prevent the pasta from sticking.*
■ *Cover the pot once the pasta has gone in: it will boil sooner. Uncover once a rolling boil has been reached or it will overflow.*
■ *Cook the pasta al dente. The instant it is cooked, drain it, add the desired sauce and serve it, unless it is going on into the oven. (see Spaghetti al Cartoccio and Lasagne al Forno)*
■ *Now see* Chef's Tips *for the home-made article.*

CHEF'S TIPS

Pasta is made simply from strong flour, water and salt, with the occasional addition of oil and eggs. The dough is child's play and, although the shapes can be rolled out by hand, I would recommend buying one of the small, stainless steel, hand-cranked pasta machines now commonly available. Since they do not get hot like electric machines, they have no tendency to dry the dough as they roll it. And in any event, making pasta by hand, though time-consuming, is highly therapeutic. Kids love to get involved, too.

INGREDIENTS (PER PERSON)

65 g/3 oz strong white flour

A pinch of salt

5 ml/1 tsp olive oil

1 beaten egg (optional)

About 60 ml/4 tbsp water

PREPARATION

■ *Sift the flour and salt together. Make a well in the middle of the flour and pour in the oil – and the egg if you wish. If you are not using egg, pour in the water.*
■ *Fold the flour and the wet ingredients together and knead thoroughly until they are well mixed.*
■ *Let the dough stand for a few minutes, wrapped to keep the moisture in. Roll out or feed into your machine.*
■ *Remember that the cooking time for fresh pasta is more accurately measured in seconds than minutes.*

Spaghetti Morgan
SPAGHETTI AL MORGAN

SERVES 6

Cooking time 45 minutes

INGREDIENTS

450 g/1 lb dried spaghetti

Salt to taste

1¼ cups/300 ml/½ pt olive oil

3 cloves garlic

1 medium onion

1 kg/2 lb fresh plum or canned tomatoes

5 ml/1 tsp sugar

1 large aubergine (eggplant)

30 ml/2 tbsp finely chopped fresh basil (one-third quantity, if using dried)

PREPARATION

■ Set to boil 4 l/7 pt water and salt it. As the water is heating, heat 60 ml/4 tbsp olive oil in a deep frying pan or skillet. Crush the garlic, slice the onions and soften them together in the oil.

■ Roughly chop the tomatoes and add them to the onion mixture when it is softened. Add the sugar and turn the heat down to simmer.

■ In a deepish pan, heat the remaining olive oil until just below smoking temperature. As the oil heats up, cut the aubergine (eggplant) into small 5mm/¼ in dice.

■ Fry the aubergine (eggplant) dice, a batch at a time, until the flesh is cooked to a wrinkled mid-brown. Set aside the cooked pieces on kitchen paper.

■ Cook the pasta until al dente; drain.

■ Stir the aubergine (eggplant) into the tomato sauce and throw in the finely chopped basil. Check the seasoning and serve with the pasta immediately.

CHEF'S ASIDE

The pungent flavour of the crisped aubergine (eggplant), and the fresh and practically uncooked strands of basil make this sauce truly special. It comes originally from Sicily, where it was probably named after the pirate.

Pasta Quills with Tomato, Bacon and Rosemary
PENNE ALL'AMATRICIANA CON ROSMARINO

SERVES 6

Cooking time 40 minutes

INGREDIENTS

450 g/1 lb penne

Salt to taste

30 ml/2 tbsp olive oil

3 cloves garlic

1 medium onion

100 g/¼ lb bacon or pancetta, roughly chopped

1 kg/2 lb fresh or canned plum tomatoes

5 ml/1 tsp sugar

30 ml/2 tsp finely chopped fresh rosemary

PREPARATION

■ Prepare the pasta in the normal manner.

■ Cook the onions, garlic in the oil as for Spaghetti al Morgan.

■ Add the bacon and sweat it for 2–3 minutes. Stir in the tomatoes and sugar. Cook the sauce for 15–20 minutes over a simmering flame. Add the rosemary to the sauce 5 minutes before serving.

■ Season and go to!

Rolled Grilled Aubergine (Eggplant) Stuffed with Spaghetti

INVOLTINI DI MELANZANE E SPAGHETTI

SERVES 6
Cooking time about 30 minutes
Oven temperature 190° C/ 375° F/Gas 5

INGREDIENTS

2 medium aubergines (eggplants)
450 g/1 lb spaghetti
Salt
60 ml/4 tbsp olive oil
3 cloves garlic
1 medium onion
1 kg/2 lb fresh or canned plum tomatoes
5 ml/1 tsp sugar
30 ml/2 tbsp finely chopped basil (one-third the quantity, if using dried)
45 ml/3 tbsp freshly grated Parmesan cheese

PREPARATION

■ *Preheat the oven. Slice the aubergines (eggplants) lengthways into 1 cm/½ in strips. Roast them as for Contorni Arrosti. (See Contorni Arrosti)*
■ *Prepare the pasta in the normal manner.*
■ *Cook half the oil together with the garlic, onion, sugar and tomatoes as for Spaghetti al Morgan. Add the basil, however, as soon as the sauce is cooked in about 20 minutes.*
■ *When the pasta is cooked, drain it and allow it to cool a little – but only a little. (If it were any hotter, it would burn you.)*
■ *Top each slice of aubergine with a thin layer of pasta. Spread tomato sauce on top of that. Roll the aubergine (eggplant) slice up into a long bundle. Secure it with a toothpick.*
■ *Arrange the bundles on a baking tray and brush them with the remaining oil. Sprinkle with the Parmesan and return to the oven and bake until the cheese forms a light crust on top of the involtini.*
■ *When serving, spoon over what remains of the sauce.*

Angry Spirals
FUSILLI ARRABIATI

SERVES 4—6

Preparation time about 25
minutes

INGREDIENTS

450 g/1 lb spiral pasta – fusilli

Salt

30 ml/2 tbsp olive oil

2 cloves garlic

1 medium onion

1 kg/2 lb fresh or canned plum
tomatoes

5 ml/1 tsp sugar

30 ml/2 tsp finely chopped
fresh basil (one-third the
quantity, if using dried)

2 fresh chilli peppers

PREPARATION

■ *Prepare the pasta in the usual manner.*
■ *Prepare a tomato sauce, using the garlic, onion, tomatoes, sugar and basil as for Spaghetti al Morgan.*
■ *As the sauce is cooking, slice and de-seed the chillies. Add them to the sauce 5 minutes before you are ready to serve it.*
■ *Drain the pasta, toss it with the sauce and carry on.*

CHEF'S TIP

Chillies leave a good deal
of their potency on the
fingers that peel them.
So be careful what you
touch afterwards – eyes,
for example – or wear
gloves.

Lasagne Baked in the Oven
LASAGNE AL FORNO

SERVES 6
Preparation time (with past'asciutta) 40 minutes
Oven temperature 220° C/ 425° F/Gas 7
INGREDIENTS
450 g/1 lb dried lasagne
Salt
60 ml) 4tbsp olive oil
2 cloves garlic
1 medium onion
1 kg/2 lb fresh or canned plum tomatoes
5 ml/1 tsp sugar
30 ml/2 tbsp fresh basil (one-third the quantity, if using dried)
600 ml/1 pt béchamel (*see* Béchamel Sauce)

PREPARATION

■ Preheat the oven. Cook the strips of lasagne until just soft in a large pot of boiling water and a little olive oil. Remove from the water, drain them, and lay them out, not overlapping, on a lightly-greased work surface.
■ Using a little over half the oil, make a tomato sauce as for Spaghetti al Morgan.
■ Grease the bottom of a 30 cm/12 in baking dish with the remaining oil. Cover it with a layer of the cooked pasta.
■ Spoon a layer of the tomato sauce onto the pasta, followed by a layer of the béchamel. Proceed thus until the dish is full: pasta, sauce, béchamel, pasta, sauce and so on. (Ensure you retain sufficient béchamel for a generous final coating.)
■ Bake in the very hot oven for 15–20 minutes, or until the top has browned well and begun to crisp at the edges.

CHEF'S TIPS

Baking pasta is a commonplace and you can do it with all kinds and with many sauces. Simply make sure the pasta is well sauced and covered or it will dry out.

Spaghetti with Clams
SPAGHETTI ALLE VONGOLE

SERVES 4
Cooking time about 25 minutes
INGREDIENTS
450 g/1 lb spaghetti
Salt to taste
450 g/½ lb fresh clams
30 ml/2 tbsp olive oil
1 clove garlic, crushed
1 medium onion, finely sliced
2 anchovy fillets, chopped
400 g/14 oz plum or canned tomatoes, roughly chopped
15 ml/1 tbsp finely chopped fresh parsley
Freshly grated black pepper

PREPARATION

■ Cook the pasta in the usual way. The sauce will take about 25 minutes, so begin it about 5–10 minutes later.
■ Put the clams in a pot with a close-fitting lid. Sweat them over a medium heat for 3–4 minutes. Remove from the heat and discard any that have failed to open. Detach the rest from their shells, rinse them to remove any sand and set aside. Strain the clam juices left in the pot and add them to the bowl with clams.
■ Heat the olive oil and add the garlic, and the onion. Soften them together for 3–4 minutes without allowing them to colour. Then add the anchovy fillets and the tomatoes. Cook the sauce for 15 minutes or so.
■ When the pasta is cooked, drain it and set it on a warm serving dish. Turn the flame under the sauce to high and, as it begins to spit, throw in the clams and the parsley. Check the salt, twist in a generous swirl of the pepper, pour over the pasta and begin.

CHEF'S TIP

It is traditional not to serve Parmesan with seafood dishes. This one is no exception.

Spaghetti Quick-Baked in Foil with Cream, Prawns and Brandy

SPAGHETTI AL CARTOCCIO CON GAMBERONI

SERVES 6
Cooking time 30 minutes
Oven temperature 190° C/ 375° F/Gas 5
INGREDIENTS
450 g/1 lb spaghetti
Salt to taste
1¼ cups/300 ml/½ pt double (heavy) cream
30 ml/2 tbsp finely chopped fresh parsley
60 ml/4 tbsp brandy or cognac
225 g/½ lb peeled uncooked prawns (cooked can be substituted, if necessary)
Freshly grated black pepper

PREPARATION

■ Preheat the oven. Set the pasta to cook in the usual manner on top of the stove.
■ As the pasta is cooking, bring the cream to boiling point in a saucepan. Add the parsley to the cream, together with the cognac.
■ Remove the cream from the heat. Let it stand so that the flavours infuse.
■ Now finely chop the prawns. If they are uncooked, add them to the cream and return it to the heat until it reboils. There is no need to bring cooked prawns to the boil.
■ When you are ready to drain the pasta, spread out on a baking tray a sheet of foil large enough to fold over and completely envelop both pasta and sauce. Place the drained pasta in the middle of the foil and pour the sauce on top. Lift the edges of the foil upwards around the pasta and fold them together, completely sealing the contents.
■ Bake the parcel in the hot oven for about 5 minutes, then transfer the foil intact to a serving dish.
■ Unseal at the table, sprinkle with black pepper and serve.

Hay and Straw with Cream and Raw Ham

PAGLIA E FIENO·CON PROSCIUTTO E PANNA

SERVES 4
Cooking time about 20 minutes
INGREDIENTS
225 g/½ lb plain noodles
225 g/½ lb green (spinach) noodles
Salt
1¼ cups/300 ml/½ pt double (heavy) cream
15 ml/1 tbsp finely chopped fresh sage
15 ml/1 tbsp finely chopped fresh parsley
⅔ cup/150 ml/¼ pt dry white white
100 g/¼ lb Parma ham
30 ml/2 tbsp butter

PREPARATION

■ *Cook the pastas in the usual way.*
■ *Bring the cream to the boil, add the sage, parsley and white wine. Keep boiling to reduce the volume of liquid by one third (i.e. to the original volume of the cream).*
■ *When this is done, dice the ham and add it to the cream. Remove from the heat.*
■ *When the pasta is cooked, drain it and whisk in the butter. Toss it in the mixture and serve very hot.*

Spaghetti with Eggs, Cream and Bacon

SPAGHETTI ALLA CARBONARA

SERVES 4 — 6
Cooking time 20 minutes
INGREDIENTS
450 g/1 lb spaghetti
Salt
6 eggs, thoroughly beaten
30 ml/2 tbsp olive oil
100 g/¼ lb Parma ham
15 ml/1 tbsp finely chopped parsley
60 ml/4 tbsp double (heavy) cream
As much freshly grated black pepper as you can take

PREPARATION

■ *Prepare the pasta in the usual manner.*

■ *Heat the olive oil and crisp the Parma ham in it. Add the parsley and cook for a minute or so over a high heat. Remove from the heat.*

■ *When the pasta is cooked, drain it. Immediately add the eggs and the ham, parsley and pan juices. Stir the spaghetti briskly so that its latent heat cooks the eggs onto the strands.*

■ *Add the cream only when the eggs have properly scrambled; the dish must on no account be too liquid.*

■ *Serve with a very generous helping of the pepper. Very hot, of course.*

Noodles with Basil, Pine-Nuts and Parmesan Cheese

TAGLIATELLE AL PESTO

SERVES 6
Cooking time about 20 minutes
INGREDIENTS
450 g/1 lb noodles
Salt
100 g/¼ lb fresh basil leaves (dried just will not do)
⅔ cup/150 ml/¼ pt olive oil
45 ml/3 tbsp pine nuts
2 cloves garlic
⅓ cup/50 g/2 oz freshly grated Parmesan cheese
45 ml/3 tbsp freshly grated Pecorino cheese (optional)

PREPARATION

■ *Prepare the pasta in the usual way.*
■ *Put all the ingredients except the cheeses in the blender; process to a fine paste. If you have no blender, you must use a mortar and pestle. In this case, add the olive oil after you have blended all the other ingredients.*
■ *Whisk in the cheeses by hand and only then check the salt: the cheeses may well be salty enough. (You may blend the cheeses along with the other ingredients, if you wish, but you will find the texture rather too smooth if you do.)*
■ *When the pasta is ready, drain it and toss it in the pesto. Mangiatelo subito!*

Thin Spaghetti with Garlic, Oil and Chilli Peppers

CAPELLI D'ANGELI AGLIO, OLIO E PEPERONCINI

Cooking time about 20 minutes

INGREDIENTS

450 g/1 lb fine spaghetti

Salt to taste

1¼ cups/300 ml/½ pt olive oil

8 cloves of garlic

4 chilli peppers

PREPARATION

■ *Plunge the pasta into about 4 l/7 pts of boiling water. Salt to taste and add a splash of olive oil.*
■ *With the remaining ingredients, make the aglio, olio and peperoncini dressing. (See Insalata di Calamaretti).*
■ *When the pasta is cooked* al dente, *drain it and toss it in the dressing. Serve immediately.*

CHEF'S ASIDE

This is *my* favourite pasta dish. Exquisite is a poor attempt to describe this Abruzzese speciality.

Dumplings with Gorgonzola
GNOCCHI AL GORGONZOLA

SERVES 4 — 6
Cooking time about 15 minutes
INGREDIENTS
450 g/1 lb potato gnocchi (*see* Chef's Tips)
Salt
1 cup/200 ml/⅓ pt milk
60 ml/4 tbsp butter
100 g/¼ lb Gorgonzola, crumbled into tiny pieces
30 ml/2 tbsp freshly grated Parmesan cheese
60 ml/4 tbsp double (heavy) cream

PREPARATION

■ *Boil the* gnocchi *as you would pasta. But watch as they will cook more quickly – 3 to 4 minutes should be quite sufficient.*

■ *As the* gnocchi *are cooking, heat the milk in a pan large enough to hold all the ingredients, including the gnocchi. As soon as the milk is warm, reduce the heat to a low simmer. Add the butter, the crumbled Gorgonzola, and the Parmesan. Slowly beat everything into a creamy paste. Remove from the heat.*

■ *As soon as the pasta is cooked, drain it and add it to the sauce. Over a very low heat, stir in the cream. Serve this luxury number instantly.*

POTATO GNOCCHI
INGREDIENTS FOR 4 — 6
675 g/1½ lb boiling – not new – potatoes
1 cup/100 g/¼ lb strong flour
Salt to taste

■ Boil the potatoes in their skins until they are just soft. Peel them as soon as you can, and blend – or mash – them while still warm.

■ Work in the flour, sifted with a little salt, until you have a pliable, sticky dough.

■ Chop the dough into thumb-sized pieces. Press each one gently with a floured fork to flatten and serrate it.

Dumplings with Chicken Livers
GNOCCHI CON FEGATI DI POLLO

SERVES 4—6
Cooking time 20 minutes
INGREDIENTS
450 g/1 lb potato *gnocchi*
Salt
30 ml/2 tbsp olive oil
2 cloves of garlic
1 small onion, very finely chopped
15 ml/1 tbsp finely chopped fresh sage
⅔ cup/150 ml/¼ pt red wine
225 g/½ lb chicken livers
⅔ cup/150 ml/¼ pt double (heavy) cream

PREPARATION

■ *Cook the* gnocchi *in the usual manner.*
■ *Heat the oil in a frying pan or skillet, throw in the whole cloves of garlic and the onion. Soften in the oil until the onion begins to brown.*
■ *Add the sage and the red wine; reduce the volume of the wine by half over a high heat. Remove.*
■ *When all the* gnocchi *are ready, bring the red wine mixture back to a boil and toss in the livers, very finely chopped. Cook for a minute or so, then add the cream.*
■ *Bring the pan back to the boil, check the seasoning and off the heat, gently stir in the* gnocchi. *Serve right-away.*

Risotto, Polenta and Pizza

Black Risotto with Cuttlefish

RISOTTO NERO ALLE SEPPIE

SERVES 4
Cooking time 25-30 minutes
Preparation 10 minutes
INGREDIENTS
1 large cuttlefish (about 1 kg/2lb)
45 ml/3 tbsp olive oil
1 large onion, finely sliced
2 cloves garlic, crushed
40 ml/4 tbsp tomato purée (paste)
⅔ cup/150 ml/¼ pt red wine
350 g/¾ lb Arborio (risotto) rice
Salt and pepper to taste
1 lemon

PREPARATION

■ *First, clean the cuttlefish. (see Chef's Tips) Make very sure you reserve the ink sac. Now slice both body and tentacles very finely indeed and set them aside. (If your fish is truly inky, the chopping board will be an interesting new colour: black.)*

■ *To soak up the excess ink peel and finely slice the onion on the same board.*

■ *Heat half the oil in a pan over a medium flame and add half the onion and the garlic, and cook both until soft. Now add the cuttlefish slices. Stir in the tomato purée and the red wine.*

■ *As the mixture cooks, either empty the ink-sac contents into it or, if the contents of the sac are hard, chop the sac and ink as well as you can. (This can be difficult, for they are often a little sticky and clinging.) Add to the pan when chopped.*

■ *Add the water in which you have cleaned the fish. (see Chef's Tips) Braise the fish mixture until the volume has reduced by about half: 25 minutes or so.*

■ *As the fish is cooking, bring 1 1/2 pt water to the boil in another saucepan.*

■ *While the water is boiling soften the remainder of the onion in the rest of the oil in another pan and add the rice. Toast it lightly .*

■ *Pour the water onto the rice and onion mixture, and boil for about 15 minutes or so until the rice is ready. Drain immediately and fold it into the fish.*

■ *Serve the cuttlefish risotto very hot, seasoned if necessary. Garnish with a bright yellow wedge of lemon — very striking against the black.*

CHEF'S TIPS

Clean the cuttlefish in as small a bowl of cold water as it and your hands will fit: it will leak ink and you will want to catch this precious substance.

To clean, hold the body in one hand and tentacles in the other. Pull gently and the two will part company. Now cut the tentacles away just above where they join the head and lay them on the chopping board. We shall return to them later. At the moment we are looking for ink.

The sac is tear-drop shaped and about the size of an average thumb. It lies at the back of the head and will be covered by a greyish-pink membrane, but its black contents will clearly show through. If ink is obscuring your view, wash the head carefully in clean water. Be careful with the sac: sometimes the contents are liquid, so cut it away over the bowl of water and let the contents fall in. Now discard the rest of the head.

The outer body is a simple business. Remove the cuttle bone — you can't miss it — and lay the flesh next to the tentacles. Pick up your best knife and start slicing.

Sound gruesome? This is an extraordinary dish. Cuttlefish ink makes the ink of the squid look like milk. But the flavour it gives to the rice is immensely subtle and perfumed. This is the best risotto I know. And certainly the most dramatic. *Buon' Appetito!*

Risotto with Dried Ceps

RISOTTO COI FUNGHI PORCINI SECCHI

SERVES 4—6

Preparation time about 20 minutes

Marinading time at least half an hour

INGREDIENTS

50 g/2 oz dried ceps (see Chef's Tips)

1¼ cups/300 ml/½ pt dry white wine

1 chicken stock (bouillon) cube (see Pastine in Brodo)

1 small onion

60 ml/4 tbsp olive oil

400 g/14 oz Arborio (risotto) rice

⅔ cup/150 ml/¼ pt double (heavy) cream

45 ml/3 tbsp freshly grated Parmesan cheese

Salt and freshly grated black pepper to taste

PREPARATION

■ Put the ceps in a pot and cover them with the white wine. Crumble the stock (bouillon) cube over them and add 4¼ cups/1 l/1¾ pt water.

■ Poach the ceps gently in the stock and wine until they are soft and swollen. Strain them carefully and reserve the poaching liquid. Wash the ceps once or twice more in fresh water: they can be gritty.

■ To remove grit from the poaching liquid, strain it too, through either muslin (cheesecloth) or a very fine strainer.

■ Boil the poaching liquid briskly. Your aim is to reduce its volume by about one third and consequently intensify its flavour.

■ As the mushroom stock boils, finely slice the onion, then soften it in a sturdy pan with the oil. Add the rice and toast it with the oil and onion.

■ Pour the mushroom liquid over the rice and let it cook until the liquid is almost absorbed. If this happens before the rice is cooked – about 15 minutes – add small amounts of water. Not too much.

■ When the rice is cooked – al dente, naturally – stir in the cream and cheese; check the seasoning. Just before serving stir in the mushrooms.

CHEF'S TIPS

Dried ceps are available in all good Italian delicatessens. As you will have gathered, the Italian for ceps is funghi porcini. They are highly prized, as well they should be.

Artichoke Risotto
RISOTTO AI CARCIOFINI

SERVES 4

Preparation time about 20 minutes

INGREDIENTS

60 ml/4 tbsp butter

1 small onion, finely sliced

350 g/¾ lb Arborio (risotto) rice

2 chicken stock (bouillon) cubes (*see* Pastine in Brodo)

2 cans artichoke hearts (*see* Chef's Tips)

60 ml/4 tbsp double cream

45 ml/3 tbsp freshly grated Parmesan cheese

Salt and Pepper to taste

PREPARATION

■ *Melt the butter in a sturdy pan. Soften the onion in it. Add the rice and toast it for 2–3 minutes. (Do not allow anything to colour.)*
■ *Crumble in the stock (bouillon) cube and add 1 ¼ l/2 pt water.*
■ *Cook the rice until it is al dente. If too much liquid remains in the pan, ladle it out.*
■ *As the rice is cooking, drain and wash the artichokes. Gently warm them with the cream and the grated Parmesan. Fold this mixture into the rice as soon as it is cooked. Season and serve immediately.*

CHEF'S TIPS

The dish originates with the baby artichokes – which can be eaten whole, choke and all – in season in Italy during very early spring. If you can find them, use them. Regrettably, they are very rare outside the country. However, they do point up a principle enshrined in the conclusion of this book, to which you are duly referred.

Risotto with Two Cheeses

RISOTTO AI DUE FORMAGGI

Preparation time about 25 minutes

INGREDIENTS

60 ml/4 tbsp butter

1 medium onion, finely sliced

300 g/11 oz Arborio (risotto) rice

2 chicken stock (bouillon) cubes (*see* Pastine in Brodo)

½ cup/50 g/2 oz fresh grated Parmesan cheese

⅔ cup/150 ml/¼ pt double cream

½ cup/50 g/2 oz crumbled Gorgonzola

Salt and freshly grated black pepper to taste

PREPARATION

■ *Melt the butter in a sturdy pan and soften the onion in it. Add the rice and toast it for 2–3 minutes.*

■ *Crumble in the stock (bouillon) and add 1 1/2 pt water. Cook the rice until it is al dente. Add the Parmesan.*

■ *As the rice is cooking, warm the cream and add the crumbled Gorgonzola to it. Stir until the cheese has thoroughly melted.*

■ *When the rice is cooked, whisk in the cream and Gorgonzola, season and serve very hot.*

How To Make Polenta
COME FARE POLENTA

SERVES 4—6

Cooking time about 30 minutes

INGREDIENTS

350 g/¾ lb coarse-grained polenta (cornmeal)

Salt

PREPARATION

■ *Bring 7½ cups/1.75 l/3 pt water to the boil in a heavy saucepan. (Polenta will tend to stick to thin pans.) Turn the water down to a simmer.*
■ *Pour the meal to run into the water in a very thin stream. (Try counting the grains!) Stir continuously.*
■ *Once all the grain has been added, keep stirring. This is a job that will take you 20 minutes.*
■ *Like couscous, the polenta is cooked when it can be lifted away from the sides of the pan as you stir. It should easily hold the shape of the spoon. Just before it reaches this point add salt.*
■ *Either serve the polenta immediately, very hot, or pour it out onto a shallow dish. When cooled and set (which takes about 2–3 hours), it can be sliced and further transformed.*

Polenta with Butter and Cheese
POLENTA CON BURRO E PARMIGIANO

SERVES 6

Cooking time about 30 minutes

INGREDIENTS

350 g/¾ lb hot, cooked polenta (*see* Polenta)

¾ cup/ 175 g/6 oz butter

⅓ cup/50 g/2 oz freshly ground Parmesan cheese

A little boiling water (about ⅔ cup/150 ml/¼ pt)

Generous amount black pepper

PREPARATION

■ *When the polenta is just cooked, pour it onto a hot serving dish.*
■ *Mix in the butter and the cheese immediately, adding a little hot water if the mixture is very thick.*
■ *Season generously with black pepper. Serve very hot.*

Grilled (Broiled) Polenta with Gorgonzola

POLENTA ALLA GRIGLIA CON GORGONZOLA

SERVES 6

Preparation time 5 minutes

INGREDIENTS

350 g/¾ lb cooked and cooled
polenta (*see* Polenta)

225 g/½ lb Gorgonzola cheese

PREPARATION

■ Cut the cold, set polenta into manageable blocks and carefully cut each block into 2.5 cm/1 in slices.
■ Heat the grill (broiler) to maximum and toast each slice on both sides, until the surface begins to brown and bubble.
■ Spread one side of each polenta slice with the Gorgonzola. Return it to the grill.
■ Serve as soon as the cheese has melted.

Fried Polenta with Mushrooms

POLENTA FRITTA CON FUNGHI

SERVES 6

Preparation time about 20 minutes

INGREDIENTS

90 ml/ 2 tbsp olive oil

30 ml/2 tbs butter

675 g/1½ lb field or wood mushrooms or ceps (*funghi porcini*), roughly chopped

2 cloves garlic, roughly chopped

2 whole small chilli peppers, roughly chopped

1 medium tomato, roughly diced

60 ml/4 tbsp red wine

15 ml/1 tbsp finely chopped fresh parsley

15 ml/1 tbsp finely chopped fresh sage

Salt and pepper to taste

PREPARATION

■ Melt one-third of the oil and the butter together over a medium flame.
■ Add the mushrooms, garlic and chillis and fry together for 3–4 minutes over a high heat.
■ Add the wine, tomatoes, parsley and sage to the mixture. Reduce the flame to a simmer.
■ As the mixture is cooking, slice the cold polenta as for grilled polenta. (see Grilled [Broiled] Polenta)
■ In a large, open pan, heat the remaining oil over a high flame.
■ Fry each slice on both sides until a thin crust forms. Keep the slices hot if you do the frying in more than one batch.
■ When all the polenta is fried, season the mushroom mixture and spoon it generously over each slice.
■ Eat it hot.

Pizza Dough
PASTA PER LA PIZZA

SERVES 6-8
Preparation time 10 minutes
Rising time 3-4 hours
INGREDIENTS
30 g/1 oz dried yeast (twice the quantity if using fresh)
1 kg/2 lb strong white flour
60 ml/4 tbsp olive oil
Salt to taste

PREPARATION

■ *Heat 150 ml/¼ pt water until it is just hot enough to bathe a baby. Add the yeast and stir well. Let the mixture stand until it begins to foam.*

■ *Pile the flour in a heap on a suitable work surface. Season it and make a well in the middle.*

■ *Have ready 600 ml/1 pt barely lukewarm water; place it alongside the flour.*

■ *Pour the yeast mixture into the well and add the olive oil. Work quickly: mix yeast, water and dough – don't use your stand-by water yet – until the consistency is even. The dough will be too dry, of course. It is now that you begin to work in the extra water. The dough should be firm and supple. Stop when you reach this point.*

■ *Now put the dough in a floured, or lightly oiled, bowl. Cover and leave in a warm place for at least three hours. When the dough has doubled in volume, it is ready to use. (There is no need to re-knead.)*

Mozzarella and Tomato Pizza
PIZZA MARGUERITA

SERVES 6-8
Preparation time 20 minutes
Oven temperature 180 °C/ 350 °F/Gas 4
INGREDIENTS
Pizza dough made with 1 kg/ 2 lb flour (*see* Pizza Dough)
450 g/1 lb fresh or canned plum tomatoes
450 g/1 lb fresh Mozzarella cheese
30 ml/2 tbsp finely chopped fresh oregano (half the quantity if using dried)
⅔ cup/150 ml/¼ pt olive oil
Salt and freshly ground black pepper

PREPARATION

■ *Preheat the oven. Divide the dough into six even portions. Roll each out to a thickness of 5 mm/¼ in.*

■ *Finely chop the tomatoes and spread them evenly over the pastry bases.*

■ *Grate the Mozzarella and spread it over the tomatoes. Sprinkle the oregano over it. Then sprinkle the olive oil over that.*

■ *Season and bake in the pre-heated oven for about 15 minutes, until the dough has risen slightly and the cheese has melted and browned.*

Pizza As You Like It
PIZZA CAPRICCIOSA

SERVES 6-8

Preparation time 30 minutes

Oven temperature 180° C/
350° F/Gas 4

INGREDIENTS

Pizza dough made with 1 kg/
2 lb flour (see Pizza Dough)

450 g/1 lb fresh or tinned
plum tomatoes

450 g/1 lb Mozzarella cheese

12 anchovy fillets

30 ml/2 tbsp capers

225 g/½ lb salami, finely sliced

225 g/½ lb mushrooms,
finely sliced

24 artichoke hearts

30 ml/2 tbsp finely chopped
fresh oregano

⅔ cup/150 ml/¼ pt olive oil

Salt and freshly ground black
pepper

PREPARATION

■ Preheat the oven. Proceed as though making Pizza Marguerita up to – but not including – the oregano-sprinkling stage.
■ Arrange even quantities of the anchovies, capers, salami, mushrooms and artichoke hearts on top of each pizza.
■ Now sprinkle with the oregano and olive oil. Season and bake for about 15 minutes.

CHEF'S TIP

Capricciosa, 'according to our whim', can be anything. Try seafood, or a variety of cheeses, or simply mushrooms, or sweet peppers. You can leave out the capers, too. I always do – can't stand the blighters.

Corn Bread with Olives
FOCACCIA

SERVES ABOUT 6

Preparation time 1 hour

Oven temperature 200° C/
400° F/Gas 6

INGREDIENTS

350 g/¾ lb strong white flour

100 g/¼ lb very fine semolina
flour

75 ml/5 tbsp fresh yeast

⅔ cup/150 ml/¼ pt olive oil

Salt to taste

⅔ cup/150 ml/¼ pt milk

50 g/2 oz green olives

PREPARATION

■ Sift the two flours together. Mix the yeast with a very little warm water. When it begins to foam, work it into the flours with a quarter of the olive oil and the salt. Blend all the ingredients very thoroughly.
■ Heat the milk. It is hot enough when bubbles begin to show around the edges of the pan.
■ Combine the milk and the flour and yeast mixture – if you have a mixer with a dough hook, so much the better. Fold in the olives.
■ Cover the dough and let it stand in a warm place for about 30 minutes. Then remove and shape into a flat round loaf.
■ Lightly oil a baking sheet with some of the remaining oil and place the loaf on it. Brush the rest generously over the dough.
■ Bake in the pre-heated oven for about 25 minutes until the top is a handsome shade of brown.

CHEF'S TIP

Eat this delectable item as hot as you can handle it. It goes superbly with a big plate of Italian hams and salamis – known as affettato misto to the cognoscenti.

Soup

Tiny Pasta in Broth 59

Rice and Peas 60

Poached Egg in Broth 61

Vegetable Soup 63

Chick-Pea (Garbanzo Bean) Soup 64

Bean Soup with Parsley, Garlic and Chilli 65

Lentil Soup 66

Potato and Onion Soup 67

Red Lettuce and Rice Soup with Fresh Sage 68

Mussel Soup 69

Tiny Pasta in Broth
PASTINE IN BRODO

SERVES 4-6
Cooking time about 3 hours
INGREDIENTS
1 medium onion
1 large carrot
2 sticks celery
1 small fennel bulb
½ medium fresh green pepper
1 medium potato
1 ripe fresh tomato (about 100 g/¼ lb)
1 kg/2 lb assorted meat scraps and bones
225 g/½ lb dried pasta stars
Salt and pepper to taste

PREPARATION

■ *Put all the ingredients except the pasta and the salt into 1.5 l/2¾ pt cold water.*

■ *Bring the liquid very slowly to just under the boil and hold it there. (Boiling makes stock cloudy, so don't.) Cook for 3 hours. Skim the broth constantly, or, when it is cooked, allow to cool and then lift off the solidified fats. (This will considerably lengthen the preparation process.)*

■ *When the broth is cooked and skimmed, add the pasta. Since you have carefully removed all the fats, you may now boil it. Do so for about 10 minutes, or until the pasta shells are just soft. Salt and serve.*

CHEF'S TIP

As I point out in the introduction, it is only the truly assiduous who teach themselves broth and stock making. For that reason, you will find frequent references to stock or bouillon cubes as you proceed. Of course, a better substitute in all cases is the home-made article and the above is how the Italians do it. You will note that it is very light and delicate. Please keep it that way – in the fridge if you wish. Use it as often as you can in place of cubes.

Rice and Peas

RISI E BISI

SERVES 4

Cooking time 20 minutes

INGREDIENTS

60 ml/4 tbsp butter

15 ml/1 tbsp olive oil

1 small onion

1 kg/2 lb fresh peas, shelled (*see* Cook's Tips)

1 stock (bouillon) cube (*see* Pastine in Brodo *Chef's Tip*)

225 g/½ lb Arborio (risotto) rice

30 ml/2 tbsp finely chopped fresh parsley

⅓ cup/50 g/2 oz freshly grated Parmesan

Salt and pepper to taste

PREPARATION

■ *Melt the oil and butter together over a low heat.*
■ *Finely chop the onion and soften it in the oil/butter mixture. Add the peas and cook them for a further 2 minutes.*
■ *Crumble in the stock (bouillon) cube and add 750 ml/1¼ pt water. Bring the mixture to the boil.*
■ *As the water (or broth) boils, add the parsley and the rice. Cook for about 15 minutes until the rice has softened but remains firm – the notorious condition of al dente.*
■ *Whisk in the grated Parmesan, season with the salt and finish with a generous twist or three of black pepper.*

COOK'S TIPS

You could use frozen peas but then why not make fish fingers? The real point of this extraordinarily simple dish is the spiky flavour of fresh peas – so cook it only when the season is right. The texture, incidentally, is midway between soup and risotto, and requires a spoon.

Poached Egg in Broth

ZUPPA PAVESE

SERVES 6

Cooking time 10 minutes

Cooking time for the broth
3 hours

Oven temperature 190 °C/
375 °F/Gas 5

INGREDIENTS

1.4 l/2½ pt light broth (*see*
Pastine in Brodo)

6 slices good Italian bread

6 eggs

45 ml/3 tbsp freshly grated
Parmesan

Salt and black pepper to taste

PREPARATION

■ Bright to the boil the broth. As the broth is heating,
toast the slices of bread to a light brown and set each in
the bottom of an ovenproof soup dish.
■ Distribute the broth evenly between the dishes.
■ Now carefully break an egg into each dish, over the
slice of bread. Do not split the yolk.
■ Put the bowls into a pre-heated oven and bake for 10
minutes or until the eggs are just set.
■ Sprinkle each with the fresh Parmesan, season and
serve.

CHEF'S ASIDE

Another dish of bare-
faced simplicity. The
broth is clearly crucial, as
is the absolute freshness
of the cheese, about
which a word: my
esteemed colleague
Georgio Raisa, a chef
from the Veneto region,
once tasted some of the
pre-grated stuff they sell
outside Italy. *'E di qual'
albero, questo?'* 'What
tree does this come
from?' he asked me. Try
this dish with duck or gull
eggs as an experiment.

Vegetable Soup

MINESTRONE

SERVES 6-8

Cooking time about ½ hour

INGREDIENTS

60 ml/4 tbsp olive oil

60 ml/4 tbsp butter

3 large onions

2 cloves garlic

225 g/½ lb carrots

2 sticks celery

225 g/½ lb potatoes

225 g/½ lb cooked white beans (*see* Zuppa di Fagioli)

100 g/¼ lb French beans

100 g/¼ lb courgettes (zucchini)

3 beef stock (bouillon) cubes (*see* Pastine in Brodo)

½ cup/100 g/¼ lb chopped fresh or tinned Italian tomatoes

⅔ cup/100 g/¼ lb piece Parmesan cheese rind

Salt and pepper to taste

PREPARATION

■ *Melt the butter together with the oil over a medium heat. Finely chop the onions, garlic, potatoes, carrots and celery and add them, one vegetable at a time, to the oil and butter in a large pot. Cook each for 2–3 minutes, without browning.*

■ *Stir in the white and French beans. Chop the courgettes (zucchini) into larger pieces and add them to the mixture.*

■ *Crumble in the stock (bouillon) cubes and stir in 1.4 l/ 2½ pt water. Stir in the tomatoes and add the whole cheese rind.*

■ *Cook the whole mixture together until you have a substantially thick soup – a consistency you must decide for yourself. Once your desire is satisfied in this matter, add water to maintain the consistency, if necessary, until the soup is thoroughly cooked – about 20 minutes. Season before serving and remember to remove the cheese rind.*

CHEF'S ASIDE

This is one version of *minestrone*. There are about as many as there are combinations of vegetables. Sometimes they contain pasta, sometimes rice and sometimes the mixture is thick with lentils. There are just two serious rules: use a lot of vegetables and don't forget the cheese rind.

Chick-Pea (Garbanzo Bean) Soup

ZUPPA DI CECI

SERVES 4-6

Preparation time about
45 minutes

INGREDIENTS

4 cloves of garlic

2.5 ml/½ tbsp dried rosemary
leaves (twice the quantity if
using fresh)

60 ml/4 tbsp olive oil

⅔ cup/150 g/5 oz canned
Italian tomatoes

450 g/1 lb tinned chick peas
(garbanzo beans), drained and
rinsed

1 chicken stock (bouillon) cube
(*see* Pastine in Brodo)

Salt and pepper to taste

PREPARATION

■ Peel and crush the garlic. If the rosemary is fresh, chop
it very finely.
■ Heat the oil and sauté the garlic until it begins to brown.
Add the rosemary and the tomatoes, roughly chopped
and lower the heat to a simmer when the ingredients
come to a boil. Cook for 25 minutes or so.
■ When the tomatoes are cooked, add the chick peas
(garbanzo beans) and cook for a further 5 minutes.
■ Stir in the stock cube and no more than 1¼ cups/300
ml/½ pt water. Season with salt and pepper to taste and
serve.

Bean Soup with Parsley, Garlic and Chilli

ZUPPA DI FAGIOLI ALL'ABRUZZESE

Preparation time 1½ hours

Marinading time 12 hours

INGREDIENTS

350 g/¾ lb dried white kidney beans

4 cloves garlic

60 ml/4 tbsp olive oil

60 ml/4 tbsp tomato pureé (paste)

30 ml/2 tbsp finely chopped fresh parsley

30 g/1 oz fresh chillies

Salt and pepper to taste

PREPARATION

▌ Soak the kidney beans in double their volume of water overnight. Leave the pot near a low heat source, a radiator or pilot light, if you can.

▌ 90 minutes before you wish to serve the soup – and that's a minimum – drain the beans, cover them with more water and set them to boil over a low heat. Cook them for between 40 and 60 minutes, until they are tender. If you are using them immediately, let them stand in their cooking water. Otherwise, drain and store covered in the fridge.

▌ Peel and crush the garlic and soften it in the olive oil over a low heat. As it begins to colour, drain away as much of the oil as you can and set it aside.

▌ Add the cooked beans, the tomato purée (paste), the parsley and no more than 300 ml/½ pt of water. Bring the mixture to the boil then lower the heat to simmer.

▌ As the soup is cooking, slice and seed the fresh chillies and stew them very gently in the garlic-flavoured olive oil until they are very soft. Pour the chilli oil into a small serving bowl.

▌ Take half the quantity of the bean soup and liquidise it. When the consistency is completely smooth, combine the two parts of the soup.

▌ Check the seasoning. The soup is now ready to serve.

CHEF'S TIP

What, you ask, is the chilli oil for? It is intended to be used as highly-spiced condiment alongside the soup. The soup has a very thick, rich consistency and a soothing flavour. The chilli oil provides a remarkable contrast.

Lentil Soup
ZUPPA DI LENTICCHE

SERVES 4-6

Cooking time about 1 hour

INGREDIENTS

30 ml/2 tbsp olive oil

1 medium onion

1 stick celery

2 slices bacon or *pancetta*

225 g/½ lb fresh or canned tomatoes

225 g/½ lb brown or green lentils

1 beef stock (bouillon) cube (*see* Pastine in Brodo)

45 ml/3 tbsp freshly grated Parmesan cheese

30 ml/2 tbsp butter

Salt and freshly ground black pepper to taste

PREPARATION

■ *In a good sized pan, heat the olive oil over a medium flame.*
■ *Very finely slice the onion and soften it in the oil. Finely slice the celery and add it to the onions when they are soft. Cook on for a further 2 minutes or so.*
■ *As the celery is cooking, dice the bacon. Add it to the mixture.*
■ *Roughly chop the tomatoes and add them to the soup, together with the lentils.*
■ *Crumble in the stock (bouillon) cube and add 1.4 l/2½ pt water. Bring to the boil on a high flame and then reduce to a simmer. You must cook the soup until the lentils are tender, up to 45 minutes. Test by tasting the soup occasionally. When the lentils are soft, season with the salt.*
■ *Off the heat, whisk in the butter and Parmesan. Pour the mixture into a suitable tureen, and generously coat the top with fresh black pepper.*

Potato and Onion Soup

ZUPPA DI PATATE E CIPOLLE

SERVES 4-6

Cooking time about
30 minutes

INGREDIENTS

60 ml/4 tbsp butter

30 ml/2 tbsp olive oil

675 g/1½ lb onions

1 kg/2 lb potatoes

1½ beef stock (bouillon) cubes
(*see* Pastine in Brodo)

45 ml/3 tbsp freshly grated
Parmesan cheese

Salt and freshly ground black
pepper to taste

PREPARATION

■ *Melt the oil and butter together over a high heat. Finely chop the onions and cook them in the oil and butter until they turn light brown. Remove the pan from the heat.*
■ *Peel and dice the potatoes and boil them with the stock (bouillon) cubes and 900 ml/1½ pints water until they are quite soft.*
■ *Now turn the potatoes and their water into the onion pan – which still contains the onions – and cook on together for a further 10 minutes. As the mixture cooks, press the potatoes into the sides of the pan to loosen any caramelised onion residue.*
■ *Stir the cheese into the soup, season and serve forthwith.*

Red Lettuce and Rice Soup with Fresh Sage

ZUPPA DI RADICCHIO CON RISO E SALVIA

SERVES 4
Cooking time 30 minutes
INGREDIENTS
45 ml/3 tbsp olive oil
1 small onion
2 cloves garlic
1 large head radicchio
1 chicken stock (bouillon) cube (*see* Pastine in Brodo)
100 g/¼ lb Arborio (risotto) rice
20 ml/1 heaping tbsp freshly grated Parmesan cheese
75 ml/5 tbsp *fresh* finely chopped sage – nothing else will do
Salt and pepper to taste

PREPARATION

■ *Heat the olive oil over a medium flame. Finely slice the onion and sauté it until it softens. It must* not *colour. Add the garlic, unchopped.*

■ *As the garlic and onions stew together, finely shred the radicchio. Add it to the pan and cook it until it softens completely – about 3–4 minutes.*

■ *Crumble in the stock (bouillon) cube and add 900 ml/1½ pints water.*

■ *Add the rice and cook everything together until the rice is cooked but still firm – yes, al dente.*

■ *Whisk in the Parmesan and the finely chopped sage. Cook on for another minute or so, 'until the dog of the herb sees the rabbit of the soup'.*

■ *Season and serve.*

Mussel Soup
ZUPPA DI COZZE

SERVES 6
Cooking time 30 minutes
INGREDIENTS
60 ml/4 tbsp olive oil
4 cloves of garlic
30 ml/2 tbsp finely chopped fresh parsley
1 chilli pepper, finely chopped
⅔ cup/150 ml/¼ pt dry white wine
225 g/½ lb fresh tomatoes
1 kg/2 lb fresh mussels

PREPARATION

■ In a pan large enough to hold everything, heat the olive oil. Crush the garlic (see *Cook's Tips*) and soften it in the oil.

■ Add the parsley and the chilli. Turn the heat to high and pour in the white wine. The pan should sizzle.

■ Roughly chop the tomatoes and add to the pan. Lower the heat to a gentle simmer and cook the mixture, covered, for about 20 minutes.

■ As the mixture cooks, carefully scrub and debeard the mussels. Discard any that are open. After 20 minutes, add them to the pan and re-cover. The soup is ready when the mussels are open – about 5 minutes. (It is unlikely you will need salt.)

CHEF'S TIPS

As to crushing garlic, you are advised to avoid garlic presses. They are a complete waste of time. The professional crushes the garlic clove firmly and progressively with the blade of a knife. This takes seconds and the knife can simply be wiped clean. Give the other thing – if you have one – to someone who doesn't cook.

Meats

Mixed Boiled Meats 71

Pot Roasted Lamb with Juniper 72

Roast Veal 73

Veal Escalope with Lemon and Parsley 75

Braised Veal Shin 75

Calves' Liver with Onion 76

Pork Pot-Roast in Milk 76

Beef Braised in Barolo 78

Fillet of Beef with Orange 79

Sausages in Tomato Sauce with Polenta 81

Cotechino Sausage with Lentils 81

Tripe with Chillies 82

Sweetbreads with White Wine,
Rosemary and Peas 85

Breadcrumbed Calves' Brains with Tomato and Basil
Dressing 85

Mixed Boiled Meats
BOLLITO MISTO

Preparation time 4 hours

INGREDIENTS

2 cloves garlic

1 medium onion

1 small fennel bulb

2 medium carrots

1 stick celery

1 large beef tomato

675 g/1½ lb ox tongue

1 kg/2 lb beef brisket joint

1 medium chicken

1 cotechino sausage

Salt

2½ cups/600 ml/1 pt *bagnetto verde* (*see* Gamberoni al Bagnetto Verde)

PREPARATION

▊ *Beg, borrow or steal a pot large enough to hold every-thing but the cotechino and the* bagnetto verde.

▊ *Put all vegetables in the pot, cover with water, and bring to the boil. Add the tongue and brisket, adjust the flame to a simmer and add more water to cover if necessary. Skim occasionally.*

▊ *After 2 hours, retrieve the tongue and remove the outer skin.*

▊ *Pop it back in the pot.*

▊ *After three hours, add the chicken. Cook the cotechino in another pot. Cook the* bagnetto verde *according to the recipe.*

▊ *After 4 hours, your feast will be ready. Simply check the salt.*

CHEF'S ASIDE

You should attempt to serve this dish all on one plate, with the meats carved and inter-leaved and the by-now fragile vegetables ranged around them. It is an extraordinary party meal. As condiments go, the *bagnetto verde* is magnificent. But the dish is also served in Italy with mustard and, surprisingly, tomato ketchup. If you *were* looking for an excuse to have a party, this dish could be it.

Pot Roasted Lamb with Juniper

ARROSTO DI AGNELLO AL GINEPRO

SERVES 4
Cooking time 2½ hours
Oven temperature 180° C/ 350° F/Gas 4

INGREDIENTS
1 large shoulder of lamb (weighing about 1 kg/2 lb)
100 g/¼ lb tritto (*see* Tritto)
1¼ cups/300 ml/½ pt dry white wine
2 good sprigs fresh rosemary
5 ml/1 tbsp juniper berries
Salt and pepper to taste

PREPARATION

■ *Heat, if available, a flameproof and ovenproof casserole. (Otherwise use a baking tray and cover it with foil later.) Heat over a medium flame without oil.*

■ *When the pan is seriously hot, drop in the lamb shoulder. Singe it for a minute on one side then turn it and do likewise. Remove it, and the pan from the heat.*

■ *Now throw in the tritto, the white wine, the rosemary and the juniper berries. Cover well and set to bake.*

■ *After 1 hour, check the liquid. Top it up to its original volume with water, if necessary.*

■ *Thirty minutes before serving, remove the lid. Season the juices with salt and pepper, and carve to serve. Could anything be simpler or more delightful?*

Roast Veal

ARROSTO DI VITELLO

SERVES 6

Preparation time about 2½ hours

Oven temperature 180° C/ 350° F/Gas 4. Pre-heat

INGREDIENTS

1 kg/2 lb shoulder joint of veal

4 cloves of garlic

2 sprigs of fresh rosemary

5 ml/1 shallow tsp of peppercorns

30 ml/2 tbsp olive oil

190 ml/⅜ pt dry white wine

Salt to taste

PREPARATION

■ *Bone the joint or ask your butcher to bone it for you. Cut out along the plane of the joint so that you can open it more or less flat on the work surface.*

■ *Crush the garlic and badly bruise the rosemary. Rub both into the inner surfaces of the meat. Roughly crush the peppercorns and sprinkle them on top. Roll the joint tightly and secure it with loops of string. Ideally find a casserole dish with a cover that is both flameproof and ovenproof. Over a highish flame, heat the olive oil in the casserole and brown one side of the joint. Turn and brown the other. Cover and begin roasting.*

■ *The joint will take some 2 hours to cook. Halfway through, turn it over completely and add the white wine. This time, when it goes back in the oven, leave the lid ajar.*

■ *For the remaining hour, you will need to check the quantity of liquid every 20 minutes or so. If it drops below half, top it up with hot water.*

■ *To serve, let the joint rest for about 10 minutes before carving. Take the string off before you slice.*

■ *Do nothing to thicken the gravy beyond boiling it a little to reduce it. Start putting flour or gravy browning in there and someone will be sure to find out about it. Then you will become the laughing stock of all your right-thinking friends.*

CHEF'S TIP

Very little could be pleasanter with this elegant roast than *spinaci conditi* (*see* Spinach with Oil, Lemon and Pepper) and some cool fried peppers. (*see* Fried Peppers with Tomato and Garlic)

Veal Escalope with Lemon and Parsley

SCALLOPINE DI VITELLO AL LIMONE

SERVES 4
Preparation time 10 minutes

INGREDIENTS
30 ml/2 tbsp olive oil
30 g/2 tbsp butter
450 g/1 lb veal for escalopes
good ½ cup/50 g/2 oz plain flour
Juice of 2 lemons
30 g/2 tbsp finely chopped fresh parsley
Salt and freshly ground black pepper

PREPARATION

■ Cut the veal into 4 equal slices and batten into escalopes. (see *Battening Meat Italian-style*)

■ Melt the butter with the oil over a high heat. Dip each escalope into the flour, shake off the excess, and fry rapidly – about 1 minute each side. Set the escalopes aside in a warm place.

■ Over a high heat, add the lemon juice to the pan juices with the parsley. Return the escalopes to the pan to warm them through – seconds only, for they are already cooked.

■ Serve instantly, seasoned as you like them.

CHEF'S ASIDE

I know we have made one or two disparaging remarks about veal escalopes elsewhere. Nevertheless, they *are* eaten in Italy, but simply. This is one simple and excellent method.

Braised Veal Shin

OSSO BUCO

SERVES 4
Cooking time 1½ hours
Oven temperature 180° C/350° F/Gas 4

INGREDIENTS
30 ml/2 tbsp olive oil
225 g/ 8 oz tritto (see *Tritto*)
4 veal shin cutlets (each weighing about 175 g/6 oz)
4 cloves garlic
1¼ cups/300 ml/½ pt dry white wine
350 g/¾ lb fresh or canned plum tomatoes, roughly chopped
30 g/2 tbp green olives, pitted and halved
2 fresh bayleaves
15 g/1 tbsp finely chopped fresh parsley
7.5 g/¼ oz thyme (fresh or dried)
Salt and freshly ground black pepper
30 g/2 tbsp finely chopped fresh basil

PREPARATION

■ Preheat the oven. Over a medium heat on top of the stove, toss the oil and tritto together until the tritto softens – about 3 minutes.

■ Increase the flame and add the veal shin steaks. Seal them well on either side. Now lift out the tritto vegetables and meat with a slotted spoon. Pour off most of the oil.

■ Replace the ingredients and, over the same high heat, add the wine, the tomatoes, the olives, the bay leaves, the chopped parsley and the thyme.

■ Bring everything to a rolling boil, then cover well. Bake in the oven for about 1¼ hours.

■ When the veal is cooked, lift it out and set it in a warm place. Boil the sauce hard to reduce its volume by about one third. Season with the salt and pepper, throw in the fresh basil, pour over the meat and serve.

Calves' Liver with Onion
FEGATO ALLA VENEZIANA

SERVES 4
Preparation time about 20 minutes

INGREDIENTS
30 ml/ 2 tbsp olive oil
6 medium onions, very finely sliced
2 leaves fresh sage
1 kg/2 lb calves' liver
60 ml/4 tbsp dry white wine
Salt and pepper to taste

PREPARATION

■ *Heat the oil and add the onions. Allow them to cook until they are soft and medium brown in colour. Roughly tear up the sage leaves and mix them into the onions when the latter are cooked.*

■ *Now remove the onions from the pan with a slotted spoon, reserve them.*

■ *Slice the liver into thin strips and increase the flame to high. Toss in the liver when the pan is very hot. As soon as each piece is sealed take the liver from the pan (see Chef's Tips) and mix it with the onions.*

■ *Return the pan to high heat and deglaze it with the white wine. When all has practically evaporated, return onions and liver to the pan, re-heat for seconds only, season and serve immediately.*

CHEF'S TIPS

You are not cooking the liver the first time out because it will continue to cook when it has left the pan. And in any event, this recipe gives you a second crack when you re-heat it. But remember, sliced finely, calves' liver literally cooks in seconds.

There is another thing the Italians frequently do with liver: *burro e salvia*. For that, clarify a large knob of butter, toss in the shredded fresh sage leaves and fry the thinly-cut liver for 30 seconds a side and no more in a very hot pan.

Very good value, this part of the book: two recipes for the price of one!

Pork Pot-Roast in Milk
ARROSTO DI MAIALE AL LATTE

SERVES 6
Preparation time about 2 hours
Oven temperature 180 ° C/ 350 ° F/Gas 4

INGREDIENTS
60 ml/4 tbsp butter
1 kg/2 lb joint of boned pork, from the loin or leg
2½ cups/600 ml/1 pt milk
Salt and freshly ground black pepper to taste
8 fresh sage leaves
2 bay leaves

PREPARATION

■ *Preheat the oven. Melt the butter over a medium heat on top of the stove in the dish you are going to use for the pork – a casserole dish with a lid if you have one.*

■ *When the butter begins to foam, add the joint and brown in on all sides.*

■ *Now slowly pour in the milk. The stream should be slow enough to boil as soon as it hits the pot. Season with the salt and pepper and throw in the sage and bay leaves.*

■ *Loosely cover the pot – with its own lid or with baking foil, if you're using a roasting tray – and consign it to the oven department.*

■ *Turn the joint completely at half time – after about 1 hour. Top up the milk at that point if the level is below half.*

■ *When the joint is cooked, let it stand for 10 minutes or so before carving. This gives you time to deal with the juices.*

■ *If the milk is still creamy and pale, boil it down until it begins to caramelize. If not, immediately add half a cup or so of water to the pan and de-glaze. (Don't be tempted to use wine or stock here. What we're after is the pure flavour of the pan juices, milk and herbs.)*

■ *Carve the meat, spoon the sauce over it and serve.*

Beef Braised in Barolo

MANZO AL BAROLO

SERVES 6

Preparation time 3 hours

Oven temperature 180° C/
350° F/Gas 4

INGREDIENTS

30 ml/2 tbsp olive oil

1 beef joint of about 1 kg/
2 lb

100 g/¼ lb *tritto* (*see* Tritto)

1¼ cups/300 ml/½ pt Barolo
or other dry red wine

1¼ cups/300 ml/½ pt broth
(use beef stock cube or *see*
Pastine in Brodo)

50 g/2 oz fresh or canned plum
tomatoes

7.5 g/¼ oz each of thyme and
marjoram

Salt to taste

PREPARATION

▌ *Preheat the oven. Heat the oil over a medium flame on top of the above and brown the joint of beef. Seal it in every possible place then set it aside.*

▌ *Now add the* tritto *to the beef pan and cook it until soft 3-4 minutes.*

▌ *Transfer the beef to a casserole a little larger than the beef itself. Retrieve the tritto with a slotted spoon – without the oil. Spread it over and around the beef. Pour in the wine, the stock and the tomatoes; add the herbs.*

▌ *Put the beef in the oven, covered with a well-fitting lid. Turn the joint completely over at half time.*

▌ *To serve, carve the joint and spoon the sauce over, checking for salt before you do.*

▌ *Watch two things: the rate of evaporation of the liquid in the pot, which you may have to top up with water, and the thickness of the final gravy. Thicken it by reducing, if you so desire. In this case, salt afterwards and not before.*

Fillet of Beef with Orange

FILLETTO ALL' ARANCIA

SERVES 4
Cooking time 20 minutes
INGREDIENTS
15 ml/1 tbsp olive oil
4 fillet steaks (each weighing about 175 g/6 oz)
60 ml/4 tbsp Marsala
60 ml/4 tbsp red wine
2 Seville oranges
Salt and a generous amount of coarsely ground black pepper

PREPARATION

■ *Heat the oil in as heavy a frying pan (skillet) as you have. Brown the steaks for a minute on each side. Retrieve them from the pan and set them aside in a very warm place. (An oven at 150° C/275° F/Gas 1 would do.) Over a very high heat, add the Marsala and red wine to deglaze the pan.*

■ *Lower the heat, zest the oranges and add both juice and zest to the pan.*

■ *If you prefer your meat medium, return the steaks to the pan and re-heat them as the juices reduce. For rare steaks, cook the wine and juice down to a consistency of light syrup before you return the meat.*

■ *To serve, pour the juices over each steak. Arrange the zest in an attractive way on top of the meat. Sprinkle with salt and a generous amount of black pepper before eating.*

Sausages in Tomato Sauce with Polenta

SALSICCIE CON POLENTA

SERVES 6

Cooking time 35 minutes

INGREDIENTS

60 ml/4 tbsp olive oil

4 cloves garlic

1 medium onion, finely sliced

450 g/1 lb fresh or canned plum tomatoes

⅔ cup/150 ml/¼ pt dry white wine

1 chilli

675 g/1½ lb uncooked continental-style sausage

335g/¾ lb *polenta* (*see* Polenta)

30 ml/2 tbsp finely chopped fresh basil

Salt and freshly ground black pepper to taste

PREPARATION

■ Heat the oil in a sturdy pan. Add the garlic and the finely sliced onion. As the onions are softening, roughly chop the tomatoes. Add them when the onion is just beginning to brown, and turn the heat to medium high.

■ Add the white wine and the chilli, and bring the sauce to the boil. Turn to a low simmer, add the sausages, and cover the pot.

■ As the sausages are braising, cook the polenta as per the recipe.

■ Sausages and polenta will be ready together. Just before you serve the one spooned generously over the other, add the finely chopped basil to the sausages and check the seasoning. More pepper than salt is my guess.

Cotechino Sausage with Lentil

COTECHINO CON LE LENTICHE

SERVES 6

Pre-preparation time 4 – 8 hours

Preparation time 2 – 3 hours

INGREDIENTS

1 cotechino sausage (*see* Chef's Tips)

30 ml/2 tbsp olive oil

4 cloves garlic

1 medium onion, roughly chopped

60 ml/4 tbsp tomato purée (paste)

⅔ cup/150 ml/¼ pt red wine

30 ml/2 tbsp fresh sage

225 g/½ lb green lentils

Salt and pepper to taste

PREPARATION

■ Soak the sausage in cold water for at least 4 hours or overnight. About 3 hours away from eating set the sausage to boil, whole and un-pricked, in plenty of water – at least 13 cups/3 l/5 pt – and start from cold. Simmer until tender – about 2½ hours.

■ With 1 hour to go, heat the olive oil to near smoking in a heavy pan. Throw in the garlic, unchopped, and the onion.

■ Cook the onion hard until it begins to catch around the edges; and then drop the flame to low. Whilst the pan is still hot, add the tomato purée (paste), red wine and the sage and stir well. Let the sage infuse in the liquids for 2–3 minutes. Add the lentils and again stir well.

■ Pour in water to cover the lentils by a 2.5 cm/1 in and cook on a low simmer until tender, about 40 minutes. Keep checking the water content. Add more to cover the lentils if you have to.

■ When the lentils are tender, let them stand to absorb whatever water remains in the pot. They should be coated with a thick, moist sheen, but should not be swimming. If there is too much liquid, increase the heat and boil it off. Season to taste.

■ Remove the cotechino from its broth when cooked. Slice and serve it on top of the lentils.

CHEF'S TIPS

You will have to find an ethnic butcher for the cotechino. On no account use already-cooked salami.

Tripe with Chillies
TRIPPA CON PEPERONCINI

SERVES 6
Cooking time about 2 hours
INGREDIENTS
1 kg/2 lb honeycomb tripe (*see* Chef's Tips)
60 ml/4 tbsp olive oil
4 cloves garlic, chopped
1 medium onion, chopped
450 g/1 lb fresh or canned plum tomatoes, roughly chopped
⅔ cup/150 ml/¼ pt dry white wine
30 g/1 oz dried ceps, washed and dried
4 chilli peppers
1 sprig fresh rosemary
2 anchovy fillets
Salt and pepper to taste

PREPARATION

■ Bring 13 cups/3 l/5 pt water to the boil and plunge the tripe into it. Boil for 30 minutes.

■ As the tripe is cooking, heat the oil, soften the garlic and onions together in it, and add the tomatoes, the wine, the ceps and 150 ml/¼ pt water. Bring everything to the boil.

■ As the sauce is warming, slice and de-seed 2 chillies. Add all chilli pieces, the rosemary and the anchovy fillets to the sauce. When it boils, turn the heat to a very low simmer and cover.

■ When the tripe has boiled for 30 minutes, remove it and slice very finely. Add it to the sauce and cook until tender enough to cut with a fork – about 1 hour. Season and serve.

CHEF'S DIGRESSION

My childhood memories of tripe in the North of England are gloomy in the extreme. I seem to recall a pale-coloured, folding substance, in texture a cross between an army blanket and a retired sponge, in flavour the very essence of a large bottle of malt vinegar. Even in the days before central heating for us sons of toil, this delicacy was always served well below room temperature.

However, such faith do I place in the Signora Olga Bernardi, the Queen of Capanna Kind, Empress of Sportinia and purveyor of matrimonial advice to myself (seated in the dining room) and the characters of Dallas (inside the TV set) that when she offered me tripe for lunch, I accepted gratefully. Not that I had any choice – she doesn't give you one.

It was terrific, of course. Needless to say, she also did what Elizabeth David characters are always doing in cookery books – throwing in a little something she just happened to find in the garden. In this case it was ceps – *funghi porcini* – which she had picked herself in the summer and preserved in oil. You can buy the same things, preserved the same way, in Italian delicatessens. They're much more expensive than the dried, but they are certainly worth considering.

Sweetbreads with White Wine, Rosemary, and Peas

ANIMELLE CON PISELLI E ROSEMARINO

SERVES 4 — 6
Preparation time about 40 minutes

INGREDIENTS
1 carrot, roughly chopped
1 stick celery, roughly chopped
2 small onions
½ lemon
675 g/1½ lb sweetbreads (see Chef's Tips)
30 ml/5 tbsp olive oil
1¼ cups/300 ml/½ pt dry white wine
350 g/¾ lb shelled peas, fresh or frozen
1 good sprig fresh rosemary
1 chilli pepper
Salt and freshly ground black pepper to taste

PREPARATION

■ Bring 2 l/3½ pt water to the boil and add the roughly chopped carrot and celery, 1 onion and the half lemon.
■ Poach the sweetbreads in the court bouillon for five minutes.
■ Remove the sweetbreads. You will now clearly see the membrane around them. Carefully remove as much of this as you can and then set the sweetbreads aside.
■ Heat the olive oil over a medium heat. Finely slice the other onion and sauté it in the oil. Add the breads, sliced into 2.5 cm/1 in chunks and brown them over a medium flame with the onions for about 3–4 minutes. Add the white wine, the peas – if using fresh ones – the rosemary and the whole chilli. Cover the pot and poach the breads for 15–20 minutes.
■ Remove the sweetbreads and set them aside.
■ Over a very high flame, reduce the cooking liquors until there will be just enough left to glaze the sweetbreads. Return them to the pan, with the frozen peas, if used. Season and serve as soon as everything is hot.

CHEF'S TIP

We are not going to tell you what sweetbreads are. Suffice it to say they are not what you think, if that is what you thought.

Breadcrumbed Calves' Brains with Tomato and Basil Dressing

CERVELLA FRITTA CON POMODORI FRESCHI

SERVES 6
Preparation time 30 minutes

INGREDIENTS
2 calves' brains
Juice of lemon
1 medium carrot
½ medium fennel bulb
1 small onion
60 ml/4 tbsp vinegar
195 ml/6 fl oz olive oil
225 g/½ lb fresh plum tomatoes
30 g/1 oz fresh basil
Salt and freshly ground black pepper to taste
3 cups/175 g/6 oz fine fresh breadcrumbs
25 ml/1½ tbsp freshly grated Parmesan cheese
2 eggs

PREPARATION

■ Soak the calves' brains in cold water and lemon juice.
■ Chop the carrot, fennel and onion roughly, bring 1 l/1¾ pt water to the boil, and add the vegetables and the vinegar.
■ Drain the brains, peel off any obvious membranous parts, and drop them into the boiling water. Poach at a low simmer for 15 minutes.
■ As the brains are cooking, divide the oil between two bowls. Skin the tomatoes and chop them roughly and finely chop the basil. Mix the tomatoes, basil, salt and pepper in one bowl of oil, and transfer to a serving dish.
■ Drain the brains, pat them dry, and set them aside in the fridge or another cool place.
■ Mix the breadcrumbs and the cheese in a shallow dish. Break the eggs and beat them in a shallow bowl.
■ Retrieve the brains from the cool place. Slice them widthways into 1 cm/½ in rounds, dip each in the egg, shake off any excess, then press each side firmly into the crumbs.
■ Fry them in the remaining olive oil over medium heat until the crumbs form a crisp crust. Serve with the tomato and basil sauce underneath.

Fish and Seafood

Trout al Carpione 87

Brochettes of Monkfish with Basil and Orange 87

Salmon or Salmon Trout Stuffed with Black Olives 88

Baked Sea Bass with Mayonnaise 89

Italian Grilled Fish 89

Grilled Scampi 90

Fried Squid 91

Braised Swordfish with Peppers 92

Braised Squid with a Parsley Stuffing 93

Salad of Fresh Tuna and Bacon from the Grill 93

Trout al Carpione
TROTA AL CARPIONE

SERVES 6

Preparation time about
45 minutes

INGREDIENTS

6 medium rainbow trout or 1
salmon trout (about
1.5 kg/3.25 lb)

1 egg

1¼ cup/300 ml/½ pt olive oil

1 cup/100 g/4 oz plain flour

1 large onion

4 cloves of garlic

⅔ cup/150 ml/¼ pt dry
white wine

30 ml/2 tbsp vinegar

30 ml/2 tbsp sugar

2 large sprigs rosemary

4 fresh bay leaves

1 chilli pepper

Salt to taste

PREPARATION

■ *Clean and dry the fish. If you are using salmon trout, cut it into slices about 1 cm/⅓ in thick.*
■ *Beat the egg and mix with its own volume of water.*
■ *Heat about one third of the oil to a medium heat, dip the whole fish or slices in the egg/water mixture and then roll in the flour. Fry gently until cooked – the whole trout 8 minutes per side, the slices 4–5. When cooking fish in this way turn it once only.*
■ *Carefully remove the fish when it is cooked and arrange it prettily on a serving dish.*
■ *Now proceed as for Aubergines (Eggplants) al Carpione. Set the rest of the olive oil on a medium heat. Slice the onion very finely and stew it in the oil. (Stew, not fry!) Add the garlic and cook both together until the onion is completely soft. Neither must brown.*
■ *Add the wine, vinegar, sugar, rosemary, bay leaves and the whole chilli. Bring everything to the boil and season. Pour the mixture over the fish and serve – warm, cool or chilled.*

Brochettes of Monkfish with Basil and Orange
SPIEDINI DI CODA DI ROSPO ALL'ARANCIA

SERVES 4

Preparation time 15 minutes

Marinading time 2 hours

INGREDIENTS

1 kg/2 lb monkfish

2 oranges

⅔ cup/150 ml/¼ pt olive oil

30 ml/1 tbsp finely chopped
fresh basil

½ cup/25 g/1 oz fresh
breadcrumbs

Salt and freshly grated
black pepper

PREPARATION

■ *Skin the monkfish and dice it into 5 cm/2 in square chunks.*
■ *Squeeze the juices from the oranges. Cut the skins into chunks about the size of the monkfish pieces and reserve. Combine the olive oil, the orange juice and the basil.*
■ *Add the fish to the marinade and scatter with the pieces of orange zest. Marinade for up to 2 hours.*
■ *Pre-heat the grill (broiler) to its maximum heat. Thread the fish onto skewers, alternating the pieces whenever you can with pieces of orange peel.*
■ *Brush liberally with the marinade once more. Sprinkle the side you are grilling (broiling) first with half the breadcrumbs. Grill (broil) for 6–7 minutes. Turn, breadcrumb the other side, and grill again. Remove the brochettes to a serving platter.*
■ *Combine any pan juices with what remains of the marinade. Bring to a rapid boil, season and pour over the fish.*

Salmon or Salmon Trout Stuffed with Black Olives

SALMONE RIPIENO ALLA PIEMONTESE

SERVES ABOUT 6
Preparation time 50 minutes
Oven temperature 180° C/ 350° F/Gas 4

INGREDIENTS
1 small salmon or large salmon trout (about 2 kg/4½ lb)
225 g/½ lb fresh or canned plum tomatoes
60 ml/4 tbsp olive oil
4 cloves garlic
2 sprigs *fresh* rosemary
6 anchovy fillets
⅓ cup/25g/1 oz black olives
30 ml/2 tbsp white wine vinegar
60 ml/4 tbsp dry white wine
30 ml/2 tbsp brandy
Salt and freshly ground black pepper to taste

PREPARATION

■ *Preheat the oven. Clean and de-scale the fish. (see Chef's Tips for Baked Sea Bass.)*

■ *Roughly chop the tomatoes and spread them out on a large sheet of foil.*

■ *Mix the olive oil with the chopped tomatoes and lay the fish on top.*

■ *Crush the garlic and smear the inside of the fish with it; lay the sprigs of rosemary and the anchovy fillets at equal intervals inside the cavity. Chop the olives very finely and sprinkle half inside, half outside.*

■ *Combine the wine vinegar and brandy and pour over the fish, then lift the sides of the foil and seal the fish carefully.*

■ *Bake the fish for 35 minutes.*

■ *Lift the fish from the foil with a long fish slice when it is cooked. Take care when transferring it so that it does not break, and set it on a serving dish.*

■ *Pour all the juices from the foil into a pan and bring them to a rapid boil. Season with the salt and pepper, pour over the fish and consume.*

Baked Sea Bass with Mayonnaise

BRANZINO AL CARTOCCIO CON MAIONESE

SERVES 6
Preparation time 35 minutes
Standing time 3-4 hours
Oven temperature 180° C/ 350° F/Gas 4

INGREDIENTS
1 sea bass (about 1.25 kg/3½ lb)
2 large onions
60 ml/4 tbsp olive oil
2 cloves garlic
2 springs rosemary
30 ml/2 tbsp finely chopped fresh parsley
30 ml/2 tbsp finely chopped fresh basil
Juice of 1 lemon
60 ml/4 tbsp dry white wine
Salt and freshly ground black pepper
2½ cups/600 ml/1 pt mayonnaise (*see* Mayonnnaise)

PREPARATION

■ *Preheat the oven. Clean and de-scale the fish (see Chef's Tips).*

■ *Very finely slice the onion and make a fish-shaped bed of it on a large piece of foil. Pour the olive oil over it and lay the fish on top.*

■ *Now crush the garlic and smear along the inside of the fish. Lay the sprigs of rosemary in there too. Chop the parsley and basil finely, mix with the lemon juice, and similarly anoint the inside of the fish.*

■ *Raise the edges of the foil, pour over the white wine and season. Seal the parcel carefully, making sure there are no holes or tears.*

■ *Set the parcel in an amply-sized dish and bake for 30 minutes. When ready, remove from the oven, but do not unseal until the parcel is completely cool.*

■ *In the meantime, make the mayonnaise.*

■ *About 45 minutes before eating, remove the fish from its wrapper and collect all the juices into a small sauce-pan. Boil them down and cool; then add them to the mayonnaise.*

■ *Decorate the fish with the onions on which it lay and serve.*

Italian Grilled Fish

PESCE ALLA GRIGLIA

SERVES 4
Preparation time 15 minutes
Standing time 2 hours

INGREDIENTS
6 whole fish (about 350g/ 12 oz each)
⅔ cup/150 ml/¼ pt olive oil
Juice of 1 lemon
Freshly grated black pepper
30 ml/2 tbsp fresh oregano
15 ml/1 tbsp very fine breadcrumbs
Rock salt to taste

PREPARATION

■ *Clean, dry and de-scale the fish, if necessary (see Chef's Tips for Baked Sea Bass). Combine the oil and lemon juice and coat the fish thoroughly.*

■ *Combine the black pepper, oregano, breadcrumbs and salt and rub into the fish. Let sit prepared for about 2 hours.*

■ *Heat the grill (broiler) to maximum heat and cook the fish, turning only once.*

Grilled Scampi

SCAMPI AI FERRI

SERVES 4

Preparation time 10 minutes

INGREDIENTS

24 large scampi
(*see* Chef's Tips)

⅔ cup/150 ml/¼ pt olive oil

Juice of 1 lemon

45 ml/3 tbsp freshly grated
Parmesan cheese

½ cup/25 g/1 oz fresh
breadcrumbs

Rock salt

PREPARATION

■ *Cut the fish in half lengthways, leaving a thin strip of shell at the back so the 2 pieces remain just attached.*
■ *Combine half the oil and the lemon juice and brush each fish with the mixture. Combine the cheese and the breadcrumbs and sprinkle over the exposed flesh. Sprinkle the fish with the remaining oil and dot with rock salt.*
■ *Pre-heat the grill (broiler) to maximum and grill (broil) until the cheese forms a light brown crust. (see Chef's Tips) Serve instantly.*

CHEF'S TIPS

Scampi is the Italian for *langoustine*, which is the French for Dublin Bay Prawn. The creatures are the same size as large Mediterranean prawns, but are distinguished from them by their prominent, lobster-like claws. They can be bought live or frozen uncooked. On no account buy cooked ones: it does not improve the flavour to cook fish twice.
As to the light brown crust, there is one way of telling when these fish are ready. You will immediately detect a rich, grilled (broiled) fish smell. Cooking time is very short, by the way. How short depends on the heat of your grill (broiler).

Fried Squid

CALAMARI FRITTI

SERVES 6

Preparation time about
15 minutes

INGREDIENTS

Scant 2 kg/4½ lb small squid

1½ cups/175 g/6 oz plain flour

Salt and freshly grated
black pepper

2½ cups/600 ml/1 pt
vegetable oil (*see* Chef's Tips)

3 lemons

PREPARATION

▌ Clean the squid (see *Chef's Tips in Braised Squid*). Slice the body sacs into rings – 5 or 6 per body for small animals.

▌ Heat the oil until it is almost smoking. Here you must use your imagination a little. You are going to fry the squid in batches small enough not to produce a serious drop in the oil temperature. If in any doubt, start with just 2 or 3 and slowly work up.

▌ Dip the squid in the flour, one batch at a time so the coating does not become soggy, shake off the excees and fry until light brown – about 30–40 seconds if the temperature is right. Set each batch to drain on paper towels.

▌ Check for salt once more when all is cooked and serve very hot, with the lemon cut in wedges.

Braised Swordfish with Peppers

PESCE ESPADA BRASATO CON PEPERONI

SERVES 4
Preparation time 30 minutes
INGREDIENTS
4 swordfish steaks (about 175 g/6 oz each)
60 ml/4 tbsp olive oil
4 cloves garlic
1 medium onion, roughly chopped
1 medium red pepper
100 g/¼ lb fresh or canned plum tomatoes, roughly chopped
1 chilli pepper
⅔ cup/150 ml/¼ pt dry white wine
Salt and pepper to taste

PREPARATION

■ *Wash and thoroughly dry the steaks. Heat the oil over a high heat and seal each steak on each side.*

■ *Remove the fish from the pan and reserve it. Turn down the heat to medium and add the whole cloves of garlic and the onions.*

■ *Turn the heat once more to high and cook the onions until the edges begin to catch. Reduce the flame to a gentle simmer and cook on until the onions and garlic are softened. In the meantime, de-seed and finely slice the peppers.*

■ *When the onions are soft, add the peppers and cook until they begin to soften – about 5 minutes. Add the tomatoes, the whole chilli and the wine. Bring to a fierce boil, then add the fish. Turn the heat to a low simmer and cover the pan, sit down (and have a glass of wine).*

■ *Simmer until the fish is very tender, about 15 minutes.*

■ *Remove the fish from the pan and set it aside in a warm place. Boil up the pan juices very briskly, until they are reduced to a thick, creamy mixture. Season, pour around the fish and serve.*

Braised Squid with a Parsley Stuffing

CALAMARI RIPIENI ALLA MARINARA

SERVES 6
Preparation time 45 minutes
INGREDIENTS
12 squid (about 8 cm/3¼ in long)
30 ml/2 tbsp finely chopped fresh parsley
2 cloves garlic, crushed
45 ml/3 tbsp freshly grated Parmesan cheese
½ cup/25 g/1 oz fresh breadcrumbs
2 anchovy fillets
1 egg
90 ml/6 tbsp olive oil
225 g/½ lb fresh or canned plum tomatoes
⅔ cup/150 ml/¼ pt dry white wine
1 chilli pepper
Salt to taste

PREPARATION

■ Clean the squid and finely chop the tentacles. (see Chef's Tips.)
■ Combine the parsley, the garlic, and the breadcrumbs. Mash and mix in the anchovy fillets.
■ Beat the egg and mix it with the bread mixture. Add about half the oil and the tentacles of the squid. Now push the mixture into the squid bodies, stopping about two thirds of the way down. (The squid will shrink as it cooks and thus push the stuffing down to the end.)
■ Heat the rest of the oil in a pan large enough to hold all the fish in one layer. Roughly chop the tomatoes and add them to the oil with the wine and the whole chilli.
■ Bring the tomatoes and wine to the boil, then turn the heat to a very low simmer. Add the squid and seal the pan tightly. Cook for about 30 minutes, until a fork will easily pierce the squid. Season the sauce and wait, if you like – this dish may be served hot, cold or in between.

CHEF'S TIPS

Cleaning squid: seize the tentacles and pull – the head and digestive businesses will follow them easily out of the tube-like outer body. Run your finger down the body to squeeze out any residue.
You will notice the tip of something that looks like a piece of transparent cellulose protruding from the body sac. This is the creature's extraordinary backbone. Thumb and forefinger will tease it out quite easily. But don't snap it: it will become difficult to reach.
Cut the tentacles away just above the point they join. Discard the rest.

Salad of Fresh Tuna and Bacon from the Grill

INSALATA DI TONNO PASSATO ALLA GRIGLIA

SERVES 4
Preparation time 20 minutes
Marinading time 2 hours
INGREDIENTS
1 kg/2 lb fresh tuna
450 g/1 lb bacon or *pancetta*
60 ml/4 tbsp fresh oregano
⅔ cup/150 ml/¼ pt olive oil
Juice of 1 lemon
2 cloves garlic, well crushed
Salt and freshly ground black pepper to taste
23 ml/1½ tbsp freshly grated Parmesan cheese

PREPARATION

■ Dice the tuna into thumb-size chunks. Lay the pancetta out in flat strips and spread it with the oregano, very finely chopped.
■ Lay a piece of tuna at the start of each bacon strip, roll in the bacon and pin with a toothpick. Continue thus down each strip of bacon until all the tuna is wrapped.
■ Combine the olive oil and lemon juice and add to it the garlic. Marinade the pinned pieces of tuna and bacon in the mixture for about 2 hours.
■ Pre-heat the grill (broiler) to its highest setting. Thread the bacon and fish chunks onto skewers. Imagine the skewers have 4 faces. Grill (broil) each face for 2 minutes – a quarter turn 4 times.
■ Detach the fish from the skewers when cooked, then separate the fish and bacon. Finely chop the bacon pieces.
■ Dress the fish in the marinade, season and sprinkle over the bacon and Parmesan. Serve warmish.

CHEF'S TIP

This dish is wonderful with the bitter taste of radicchio. Shred two heads and serve the salad on top.

Chicken and Game

Italian Grilled Chicken 95

Italian Roast Chicken with Rosemary 96

Chicken Braised with Bacon, Onion and
Red Peppers 96

Papardelle Noodles with Tomato Sauce and
Hare Stock 98

Rolled and Pot-Roast Hare 99

Rabbit with Onions 101

Roast Rabbit with Lamb 101

Pigeon Breasts with Pine-nuts and Lemon 102

Pheasant Braised with Three Alcohols 103

Italian Grilled Chicken

POLLO ALLA DIAVOLA

SERVES 4
Preparation time 30 minutes
Marinading time 2 hours
INGREDIENTS
1 roasting chicken (weighing about 1.25 kg/2½ – 3 lb
Juice of two lemons
⅔ cup/150 ml/¼ pt olive oil
15 ml/1 heaped tbsp peppercorns
Rock salt to taste

PREPARATION

■ Take a large pair of scissors to the chicken's backbone and cut it out. Lay the bird breast side up on your work-top and press down onto the breast to flatten it. Now cut diagonal slashes across the breasts and thighs.

■ Set the chicken in a dish and pour over it the lemon juice and olive oil. Very roughly crush the peppercorns and sprinkle them over the chicken. Let it marinade for about two hours.

■ Pre-heat the grill (broiler). It should be as hot as possible.

■ After marinading, sprinkle the chicken breasts liberally with the rock salt. Grill (broil) until the breasts turn light brown. Turn the chicken over. Pour some of the marinade into the cavity and grill (broil) on for a further 10 minutes.

■ Turn once more, baste with the marinade (scoop up the juices from the grill (broiler) pan, too), and remove when the whole bird is a fetching mid-brown.

Italian Roast Chicken with Rosemary

POLLO ARROSTO CON ROSMARINO

SERVES 4
Preparation time 1 hour or so
Oven temperature 190° C/ 375° F/Gas 5
INGREDIENTS
1 roasting chicken (about 1.25 kg/2½ – 3 lb
4 cloves garlic
4 good sprigs fresh rosemary
⅔ cup/100 g/4 oz *tritto* (*see* Tritto)
60 ml/4 tbsp olive oil
60 ml/4 tbsp dry white wine
Salt to taste

PREPARATION

■ *Preheat the oven. Put the chicken in a roasting tin, crush the garlic roughly and smear it around the cavity of the chicken, and put 2 sprigs of rosemary inside with it, then chop the remainder and sprinkle it over and around the bird with tritto and oil. Commit the whole ensemble to the oven.*

■ *The chicken will be cooked in an hour or so, but baste it thoroughly with the pan juices every 15 minutes.*

■ *When cooking is complete, let the bird rest for 5 minutes or so. Skim the oil off the pan juices and set the dish over a very hot flame. Add the wine and bring everything to a rapid boil. Season, pour over the chicken and serve.*

Chicken Braised with Bacon and Red Peppers

POLLO CON PEPERONI E PANCETTA

SERVES 4
Preparation time 45 minutes
INGREDIENTS
1 roasting chicken (about 1.25 kg/2½ – 3 lb)
60 ml/4 tbsp olive oil
4 sweet red peppers
4 cloves garlic
4 chilli peppers
225 g/½ lb bacon or *pancetta*
Salt to taste

PREPARATION

■ *Joint the chicken into 4 pieces. Heat the oil in your heaviest casserole – one with a good lid – and thoroughly brown the chicken pieces. Remove them from the heat.*

■ *Deseed the red peppers and slice into fine strips. Cook until soft in the chicken oil – about 10 minutes. Return the chicken pieces to the pan, smothering them with the peppers.*

■ *Add the whole garlic and the whole chillies. Lay the strips of bacon over everything, cover the pan and cook at a very low heat until the chicken is tender – about 30 minutes.*

■ *Season lightly with the salt. (Remember that with the bacon, you will need little.)*

CHEF'S ASIDE

This is a dish that is remarkably easy to spoil. The whole point of it is that the chicken cooks in its own juices, flavoured simply by the peppers. No onions. No other stock. The bacon on top provides the lubrication required. Splendid.

Papardelle al Sugo di Lepre

INGREDIENTS

600 ml/1 pt stock made from the bones, kidneys and heart of a hare (*see* Pastine in Brodo, but substitute hare bones)

1¼ cups/300 ml/½ pt tomato sauce (*as for* Spaghetti al Morgan but without the fried aubergines)

225 g/½ lb papardelle noodles

1 hare liver

PREPARATION

■ *Combine the stock and the tomato sauce. Reduce both until the volume is halved.*
■ *Prepare the pasta in the usual manner. (see Pasta)*
■ *Immediately before serving, mash the hare liver very finely and stir it into the very hot pasta sauce. A rich and succulent dish.*

CHEF'S TIP

This dish properly belongs in the Pasta section. However, I could not bring myself to write, under ingredients, anything quite so bizarre as 'the bones, liver, kidneys and heart of a fresh hare'. These are not items you can go out and buy. You rather acquire the animal itself and then find yourself stuck with them.

But you will not be stuck. This dish of Paypardelle — broad, thin noodles up to 2 cm wide — is a Piedmontese speciality and delicious.

Rolled and Pot-Roast Hare

LEPRE AL ROTOLO

SERVES 6–7
Preparation time 2 hours
Oven temperature 180° C/ 350° F/Gas 4
INGREDIENTS
1 large hare
225 g/½ lb unsmoked bacon or *pancetta*, the fattier the better
2 cloves garlic
20 ml/1 heaping tbsp crushed fresh rosemary (half the quantity, if using dried)
20 ml/1 heaping tbsp crushed fresh thyme (half the quantity, if using dried)
20 ml/1 heaping tbsp crumbled fresh sage (half the quantity, if using dried)
60 ml/4 tbsp olive oil
Juice of 1 lemon
225 g/½ lb tritto (*see* Tritto)
225 g/½ lb fresh or canned plum tomatoes
25¼ ml/½ pt dry white wine
Salt and freshly ground pepper to taste

PREPARATION

■ *Preheat the oven. Remove the hare's legs. Cut through the meat along the line of the bones and remove the bones. Set them aside. Batten each of the legs into an escalope about 1 cm/⅓ in thick. (see* Battening Meat Italian-style)

■ *When all four leg escalopes are nicely flat, arrange them together, with their adjoining edges overlapping slightly, so they form a rough rectangle. (Just to keep you in the picture, you are going to lay strips of meat along the longer edge of this rectangle and then roll the thing up, Swiss-roll-style.)*

■ *Now for the strips of meat. Running along the back of the hare – the saddle – are two thin, round strips of meat (the sirloins) and they stretch from the shoulder blades to the haunch. Run the point of a sharp knife along the top of the saddle, very close to the spine, from front to rear. This will free one sirloin from the back. Push/roll the meat down over the ribs. Cut it free as soon as there is no more meat between the skin and ribs. Pull or cut off the skin and set aside.*

■ *Lay the first sirloin along the rectangle of escalopes. Do the same with the other sirloin. Lay the bacon in long strips around the sirloins.*

■ *Cut free the fillets (the tiny triangular strips of meat on the inner side of the ribs towards the haunch and slot them into the meat strips wherever they will fit.*

■ *Roughly crush the garlic and all the herbs and rub them into the leg meat and sirloins. Pour over half the olive oil and the lemon juice and complete the filling with half the tritto.*

■ *Roll up the outer leg meat so the whole hare now re-sembles a fat and untidy sausage. Secure it with loops of string.*

■ *In as tight-fitting a casserole dish as you can find, brown the tritto in the remaining oil. Add the hare sausage and brown it evenly. Roughly chop the tomatoes and add them and the wine to the dish.*

■ *Cover and bake in the oven for about 1½ hours, or until the hare is very tender.*

■ *Season the pan juices, carve the roulade and serve the juices spooned over it. You will have first thoughtfully removed all trace of string.*

Rabbit with Onions

CONIGLIO ARROSTO CON CIPOLLE

SERVES 4
Cooking time 1½ hours
Oven temperature 180° C/ 350° F/Gas 4

INGREDIENTS
1 large rabbit (weighing about 1 kg/2 lb)
60 ml/4 tbsp olive oil
3 large onions
6 cloves garlic
6 bay leaves
3 chilli peppers
4 good sprigs fresh rosemary
60 ml/4 tbsp brandy
Salt and freshly grated black pepper to taste

PREPARATION

■ *Preheat the oven. Cut away the legs from the rabbit carcase and joint each one once more at the knee. Cut the saddle into 4 pieces: haunch, belly and the rib cage, split in two along the breast bone.*

■ *Heat the oil over a medium heat and brown the rabbit pieces for 3–4 minutes. Remove them with a slotted spoon and set aside.*

■ *Slice the onions very finely and add them to the rabbit pan. Increase the heat and cook them until they begin to colour. Reduce the heat and add the whole garlic, the whole chillies and the whole sprigs of rosemary.*

■ *Return the rabbit to the pan and smother with the onions. Cover tightly and begin baking.*

■ *After about 1 hour, completely turn all the contents, add the brandy and season. Continue cooking until the rabbit is very tender – another 30 minutes or so.*

CHEF'S ASIDE
How versatile is the rabbit! A cuddly, trouble-free household pet that will eat practically anything you give it, bar your fingers. And notwithstanding, a source of delight and simple pleasure to gastronomes the world over. Would we could say the same about cats.

Roast Rabbit with Lamb

CONIGLIO ARROSTO CON AGNELLO

SERVES 8–10
Preparation time 2 hours
Oven temperature 180° C/ 350° F/Gas 4

INGREDIENTS
1 large lamb shoulder (weighing about 2 kg/4½ lb), cut into 8 large bone-in chunks
1 large rabbit, jointed into 8 – 4 legs with the saddle cut into 4 pieces.
1 large onion, sliced
4 cloves garlic, roughly crushed
4 good sprigs rosemary
12 fresh sage leaves
1¼ cups/300 ml/½ pt dry white wine
60 ml/4 tbsp dry Marsala
Salt and freshly ground black pepper to taste

PREPARATION

■ *Preheat the oven. Heat a baking tray to very hot. Add no oil. (There's none in the recipe, so you can't!) Drop in the lamp shoulder. Seal the lamb pieces by sautéeing very fiercely, then lower the heat until a little of the lamb fat begins to run. Remove the lamb and set aside.*

■ *Add the jointed rabbit. Seal the rabbit gently for 2–3 minutes. Remove and set aside.*

■ *Scorch the onion in what should be a very lightly-greased baking tray. Add the garlic, rosemary, sage and the wines. Bring everything to the boil.*

■ *Replace the meat, making sure the pieces alternate with each other: the fat of the lamb must moisten the rabbit during the cooking process and the flavour of the rabbit must permeate the lamb. Season at this point.*

■ *Cover and bake in the oven for about 1½ hours.*

CHEF'S ASIDE
This reasonably cunning combination links two meats with very different, but highly complementary, basic qualities. The result is extremely interesting. You could just squeeze by with half a shoulder and half a rabbit if you want to cook for a smaller number but, really, bulk is best: the juices flow faster and stronger.

Pigeon Breasts with Pine Nuts and Lemon

PETTI DI PICCIONCINI AL LIMONE E NOCCE DI PINI

SERVES 4

Preparation time 45 minutes

INGREDIENTS

6 young pigeons

60-75 ml/¼/⅓ cup *tritto*
(*see* Tritto)

⅓ cup/50 g/2 oz pine nuts

60 ml/4 tbsp olive oil

Juice and zest of 1 lemon

⅔ cup/150 ml/¼ pt Marsala
wine

PREPARATION

◾ *Remove the breasts from the pigeons. Keeping the blade very close to the high-ridged breast bone, a swift stroke of the knife from back to front will have the breast hanging on by skin only. Cut through the skin.*

◾ *Brown the tritto in a very large pan. Roughly chop the carcasses. As the tritto browns, add them, cover with water and bring to the boil. Allow to simmer.*

◾ *In a frying pan (skillet) containing no oil, toast the pine kernels until they begin to brown. Remove them from the heat immediately – they will continue to cook a little of their own accord.*

◾ *Heat the olive oil in a heavy pan and drop in each pigeon breast. Cook for no more than 10 seconds on each side. The breasts will puff up. Remove the skin then slice each breast through across the horizontal – i.e. flat – plane. Seal the raw sides of each breast for a further 2–3 seconds in the hot oil.*

◾ *Pour away most of the oil and return the pan to a high heat. Add the lemon juice, zest and the Marsala and reduce until you have a thick syrup, about 5 minutes. Stir in ⅔ cup/150 ml/¼ pt of the pigeon broth made from the carcasses and reduce again.*

◾ *Toss the breasts into the sauce and re-heat for half a minute. Remove the breasts from the pan, pour the sauce over them, and sprinkle the browned pine nuts on top.*

CHEF'S TIPS

The pigeon breasts take no time at all to cook. Very hard and very fast is the golden rule here. They will be excessively tender.

This recipe also wins you some extra pigeon stock, with which you can, if you wish, make a pasta sauce much along the lines of Papardelle al Sugo di Lepre. Of course the smaller pigeons yield rather less stock.

Pheasant Braised with Three Alcohols

FAGIANO BRASOTO AI TRE VINI

SERVES 4
Preparation time 2½ hours
Oven temperature 170° C/ 325° F/Gas 3

INGREDIENTS
2 pheasants
60 ml/4 tbsp olive oil
1 medium onion, finely sliced
2 cloves garlic
8 sprigs of fresh rosemary
60 ml/4 tbsp Marsala
60 ml/4 tbsp brandy
⅔ cup/150 ml/¼ pt dry white wine
Salt and freshly ground black pepper to taste

PREPARATION

■ *Preheat the oven. Cut away the backbones, then slice each bird into two: cut down through the centre of the breastbone.*

■ *In a tray large enough to hold the halves side by side, heat the oil. Soften in it the finely sliced onion. Throw the garlic in whole.*

■ *As the onion cooks, flatten out the pheasants as much as you can. Either press quietly and discreetly with the palm of your hand or work them over brutally with the flat of a cleaver. The latter is more fun, especially in a top floor apartment.*

■ *Lay the sprigs of rosemary on top of the softened onions then lay the pheasant breasts down on top of that. Cook thus for 2–3 minutes on a high flame.*

■ *Take a fork and liberally prick the upper and still un-cooked sides of the birds. Mix the Marsala and brandy together and pour an equal amount over each bird.*

■ *Cover the dish very tightly and commit to the oven.*

■ *After 1½ hours cooking, turn the birds, scooping all the onion and rosemary you can onto the tops of the breasts. Now add the white wine.*

■ *Return once more to the oven and continue cooking until the pheasants are very tender – about 1 hour more.*

■ *Season the pan juices at the last minute and pour on top of the birds.*

CHEF'S TIP

The dish in which you cook these birds should be a perfect fit for them. If it is a little large, check the liquid levels a couple of times and moisten if necessary. A second possibility in the case of an oversize dish is bacon – 225 g/½ lb draped over the birds will help.

Vegetables and Omelets

Aubergines (Eggplants) Al Carpione

MELANZANE FRITTE AL CARPIONE

SERVES 4

Preparation time 20 minutes

INGREDIENTS

1¼ cups/300 ml/½ pt olive oil

1 large onion

4 cloves garlic

⅔ cup/150 ml/¼ pt dry white wine

60 ml/4 tbsp vinegar

30 ml/2 tbsp/sugar

2 large sprigs fresh rosemary

4 fresh bay leaves

1 chilli pepper

2 medium aubergines (eggplants)

Salt to taste

PREPARATION

■ *Put half the olive oil in a pan and set it over medium heat.*
■ *Slice the onion very finely and stew it in the oil. (Stew, not fry). Add the garlic and cook both together until the onion is soft. It must not colour.*
■ *Add the wine, vinegar, sugar, rosemary, bay leaves and the whole chilli. Bring the mixture to the boil, then remove it from the heat and season it. Reserve.*
■ *Cut the aubergines (eggplants) into ½–4 cm/¼–1½ in batons and fry them in batches in the remaining oil over a high-ish heat. Cook them until they wrinkle and brown severely.*
■ *Set each batch to drain on paper towels as you undertake the next.*
■ *When all aubergine (eggplant) is cooked, arrange it in a dish.*
■ *Simply pour the wine and oil mixture over it, stand back and marvel.*

CHEF'S ASIDE

This dish, with the wizened chocolate colour of the fried aubergines (eggplants) covered by the slender, pale strands of onion, whole clumps of rosemary, dangerous-looking pieces of garlic and the sheen of the oil and wine, looks utterly magnificent. It tastes even better.

Aubergines (Eggplants) Baked with Garlic Sott'olio

MELANZANE AL FORNO SOTT'OLIO

SERVES 4—6
Preparation time 15 minutes
Oven temperature 200° C/ 400° F/Gas 6
INGREDIENTS
2 large aubergines (eggplants)
4 cloves garlic
⅔ cup/150 ml/¼ pt olive oil
Juice of half a lemon
Salt and freshly ground black pepper

PREPARATION

■ Preheat the oven. Cut the spiky stalk off the aubergines (eggplants). Peel the garlic cloves and cut them lengthways into thinnish slivers.

■ Pierce the aubergines (eggplants) all over with a thin-bladed knife. Push the slivers of garlic into the slits.

■ Place the aubergines directly onto the wire shelving of the oven. Do not oil them in any way. Bake for 15 minutes, until the vegetables shrink into themselves and the skins wrinkle. When cooked, they will feel soft to the touch.

■ Remove the aubergines (eggplants) from the oven and allow them to stand for 3–4 minutes.

■ Slice them into neat, thin, strips lengthways. Dress them with the oil, lemon juice, salt and pepper.

■ Serve hot, warm or cool.

CHEF'S ASIDE

The simplest is the best. Cooked in this way, the aubergines (eggplants) steam in their own juices, hermetically sealed by their skins. The flavoured steam also picks up the scent of the garlic and forces it through the plant. Magnificent. Another lovely dressing would be *Aglio, olio e peperoncini.* (*see* Insalata di Calamaretti and Spaghetti Aglio, Olio e Peperoncini)

Baked Aubergines (Eggplants) with Mozzarella

MELANZANE ALLA PARMIGIANA

SERVES 4
Preparation time about 30 minutes
Oven temperature 200° C/ 400° F/Gas 6
INGREDIENTS
2 medium aubergines (eggplants)
60 ml/4 tbsp olive oil
450 g/1 lb fresh or canned plum tomatoes
30 ml/2 tbsp fresh oregano (half the quantity for dried)
Salt and freshly ground black pepper
225 g/½ lb Mozzarella cheese
45 ml/3 tbsp freshly grated Parmesan cheese

PREPARATION

■ Preheat the oven. Cut off the coarse stalks of the aubergines (eggplants) and slice them lengthways in 1 cm/½ in slices. Bake the slices in the oven, directly on the wire shelving, for 10 minutes or until very soft.

■ In the meantime, oil a baking dish. Chop the tomatoes roughly and combine with the oregano. Season strongly with the salt and pepper. Grate the Mozzarella and mix it with the Parmesan.

■ Remove the aubergine (eggplant) slices from the oven and line the baking dish with one layer. Spread the tomato and oregano mixture evenly over it, and sprinkle the Mozzarella and Parmesan on top of that. Continue these layers until the dish is full, leaving yourself a good amount of Mozzarella and Parmesan as a final, thick coating: the cheese will melt and seal the dish as it cooks.

■ Bake until the cheese melts and browns – 15–20 minutes.

Fried Peppers with Tomato and Garlic

PEPERONATA

SERVES 4
Cooking time 20 minutes
INGREDIENTS
6 medium peppers, 3 red and 3 green
60 ml/4 tbsps olive oil
3 cloves garlic, crushed
175 g/6 oz fresh or canned plum tomatoes
Salt to taste

PREPARATION

■ Halve and de-seed the peppers and slice cross-wise into 6 mm/¼ in strips.

■ Heat the oil in a shallow pan large enough to hold all the peppers confortably. Add the peppers and the crushed garlic cloves. Cook over medium heat until the peppers begin to soften.

■ As the peppers cook, roughly chop the tomatoes. If they are fresh, skin them. Add the tomatoes to the peppers in the pan, cover, and reduce the flame to simmer.

■ Season when the peppers have softened completely – about 15 minutes. Serve hot, warm or cold.

Spinach with Oil, Lemon and Pepper

SPINACI CONDITI

SERVES 4—6
Cooking time 15 minutes
INGREDIENTS
1 kg/2 lb fresh spinach
⅔ cup/150 ml/¼ pt olive oil
Juice of half a lemon
Salt and a copious quantity of freshly ground black pepper

PREPARATION

■ Trim the stalks from the spinach leaves. (see Chef's Tips)

■ Very lightly oil the bottom of a thick pan and set in on a low heat. Introduce the spinach a little at a time. It will shrink as it comes in contact with the heat. Cover the pan and steam the spinach for about 10 minutes over a fairly low heat.

■ When the spinach is cooked, press it lightly in a colander and secure the juices for another use. (see Chef's Tips) Allow the spinach to cool slightly. Then simply dress it with the olive oil, lemon juice, salt and pepper.

■ Eat it hot, warm or cool.

CHEF'S TIPS

You can make soup with the spinach stalks, as you can with the juices of the spinach, if you go to the trouble of keeping it for later use, either in the refrigerator or in the freezer.

Fennel Milanese Style

FINOCCHIO MILANESE

SERVES 4—6
Preparation time 25 minutes
INGREDIENTS
3 medium fennel bulbs
⅔ cup/150 ml/¼ pt white wine
30 ml/2 tbsp vinegar
1 clove garlic
2 bay leaves
Salt to taste
2 eggs
3 cups/175 g/6 oz fresh breadcrumbs
⅔ cup/150 ml/¼ pt olive oil

PREPARATION

■ The fennel, though bulb-like, is also slightly flattened. So cut it into 6 mm/¼ in slices from the root upwards, in the same plane as its flat side. You will find that the inner 3 or 4 slices hang together as cross-sections of the plant. Set all these aside.

■ Put the rest, with the white wine, vinegar, garlic and bay leaves, into 1 1/2 pt water, and bring everything to the boil. Salt the liquid to taste and poach the fennel cross sections in it for 10–15 minutes or until soft. (see Chef's Tips) Drain the fennel and pat it dry.

■ In a shallow bowl, beat the two eggs well. Dip each fennel piece into the egg, covering it well. Shake off any excess. Now press the fennel slices forcefully into the breadcrumbs, spread out on an open surface to facilitate the process.

■ Heat the oil to a fast-frying temperature; fry each fennel slice until crisp on both sides. Eat hot.

CHEF'S TIPS

Poaching liquids like this can often come in handy. There is no reason, therefore, why you should not strain them after use and keep them chilled or frozen. Incidentally, if you are going to ask about this dish in Italy, watch how you go about it. *Finocchio* is also Italian slang for homosexual!

Pronunciation note: the word is pronounced 'fin-ock-ee-o!'. You will see that 'cch' comes out as an English 'k'. (So does 'ch', as it happens.) Now for the exam. How do you pronounce 'radicchio'? (*see* Zuppa di Radicchio con Salvia)

Broccoli with Green Pepper and Garlic
BROCCOLI ALL'AGLIO E PEPERONI VERDI

SERVES 4—6
Preparation 6–8 minutes
INGREDIENTS
675 g/1½ lb fresh broccoli
Salt to taste
30 ml/1 fl oz olive oil
1 small green pepper, deseeded and finely sliced
4 cloves garlic
12 ml/¾ tbsp freshly grated Parmesan cheese
Freshly grated black pepper

PREPARATION

■ Bring plenty of salted water to the boil drop in the trimmed broccoli florets and boil for 3 minutes. Drain them and stop the cooking process by plunging them in cold water.

■ Heat the olive oil over a high flame. Cook the pepper in the oil until the slices begin to brown slightly at the edges. Reduce the heat to a simmer and add the garlic cloves, well crushed. Cook the pepper and garlic together for 1–2 minutes.

■ Add the broccoli and the Parmesan, turn in the oil and Parmesan until the broccoli is hot.

■ Serve immediately, lavishly sprinkled with the pepper.

CHEF'S TIP

The Parmesan is as much for grain as for taste — hence the small quantity.

Gratinéed Jerusalem Artichokes
TOPINAMBURI GRATINATI

SERVES 4—6
Preparation time 15-20 minutes
Oven temperature 200° C/ 400° F/Gas 6
INGREDIENTS
450 g/1 lb Jerusalem artichokes (see Chef's Tips)
Salt
60 ml/4 tbsp butter
45 ml/ 3 tbsp freshly grated Parmesan cheese
Freshly grated black pepper

PREPARATION

■ Preheat the oven. Scrub the artichokes in a robust fashion and cut away any darker patches of skin. (There is no need to peel them, unless you have all week.)

■ Drop the artichokes in boiling salted water – cover well – and cook for 10 minutes. They should be firm but easily biteable. Remove them from their cauldron, drain and slice thinly.

■ Grease a baking dish with a little of the butter and layer it with the artichokes. Dot the rest of the butter over the top.

■ Sprinkle with the Parmesan and a stiff measure of pepper. Bake them until the cheese and butter form an enticing brown crust. Serve very hot.

CHEF'S TIPS

These artichokes are, as you probably know, nothing to do with the other sort. On a further point of information, they resemble heavily mis-shapen potatoes or fresh root ginger. Their unique and delectable flavour makes splendid soups, especially when puréed with chicken stock.

Courgettes Fried in Light Batter

ZUCCHINI FRITTI CON LA PASTELLA

SERVES 4
Cooking time 6–10 minutes
INGREDIENTS
450 g/1 lb courgettes (zucchini)
1 cup/100 g/¼ pt plain flour
Salt and pepper to taste
1¼ cups/300 ml/½ pt vegetable oil

PREPARATION

■ *Slice the courgettes (zucchini) into batons approximately 1 cm/½ in thick and 5 cm/2 in long, depending on the size of the individual vegetables.*

■ *Sift the flour with the salt and pepper, then mix it very gradually with water, beating constantly to avoid lumps. Stop when your batter is the consistency of thick cream.*

■ *Heat the oil until very hot, dip the courgettes (zucchini) in the batter, and then fry in batches — they should fit only loosely into the pan. When the batter is crisp and brown, the vegetables are ready.*

■ *Like all fried food, they should be served very hot.*

CHEF'S TIP

It is sometimes difficult to recommend quantities of oil in cases like this. Since this recipe requires deep frying, the depth, with a fixed volume of oil, will clearly vary with the diameter of the pan. Bear in mind that there should be enough oil for the sliced courgettes (zucchini) to float.

Mushrooms Fried with Garlic and Parsley

FUNGHI TRIFOLATI

Cooking time about 5 minutes

INGREDIENTS

675 g/1½ lb good mushrooms
(*see* Chef's Tips)

60 ml/4 tbsp olive oil

3 cloves garlic, crushed

30 ml/2 heaping tbsp chopped
fresh parsley

Salt and freshly ground black
pepper to taste

PREPARATION

■ *Wash but do not peel – never peel – the mushrooms. Slice or chop them into thumb-sized chunks if they are particularly large.*
■ *Heat the oil to medium and sauté the crushed garlic for 30 seconds or so. Add the mushrooms. These will absorb the oil very promptly. When they do, turn down the heat and wait for the process to reverse – the mushrooms begin to give off their own liquor. This will take 2 minutes or so.*
■ *Increase the heat and add the parsley, salt and pepper. Cook on for a further 2–3 minutes and serve.*

CHEF'S TIPS

The Italian verb 'to fry with garlic and parsley' is *trifolare* and you will find quite a number of things *trifolati* – courgettes (zucchini) for example. And what is a good mushroom? What is *not* a good mushroom is that small, white, perfectly symmetrical item that looks like a children's storybook illustration.

Spinach and Ham Omelet

FRITTATA DI SPINACI E PROSCIUTTO

Before we get down to business here, a word about the Italian omelet. It is not the light and runny affair of France but a thick, multi-egged and completely cooked number, served in wedges like a cake, often cold. Such dishes may be eaten at the evening meal, which in Italy is traditionally much lighter than lunch.

SERVES 4
Preparation time 20 minutes
INGREDIENTS
6 eggs
45 ml/3 tbsp freshly grated Parmesan cheese
100 g/¼ lb Parma ham, roughly chopped
175g/6 oz cooked spinach (*see* Spinaci Conditi)
Salt and pepper to taste
30 ml/4 tbsp olive oil

PREPARATION

■ *Thoroughly beat the eggs. Mix in the cheese, ham, spinach, salt and pepper.*
■ *Heat the oil over a medium flame, in as heavy a pan as you have. Pour in the mixture and then turn the heat down as low as it will go. Cover the pan and cook until everything is set – about 20 minutes.*
■ *Serve at whatever temperature you wish.*

Tomato, Onion and Basil Omelet

FRITTATA CON POMODORI, CIPOLLE E BASILICO

SERVES 4
Preparation time 30 minutes
INGREDIENTS
60 ml/4 tbsp olive oil
1 medium onion, finely chopped
225 g/½ lb fresh or canned plum tomatoes
45 ml/3 tbsp roughly chopped fresh basil
6 eggs
45 ml/3 tbsp freshly grated Parmesan cheese
Salt and pepper to taste

PREPARATION

■ Heat a little over half the oil in a heavy pan. Add the onions and cook until soft – about 3–4 minutes.
■ As the onions are cooking, roughly chop the tomatoes. Add them when the onions are ready. Turn up the heat and reduce the pan liquids by a good third.
■ Toss in the roughly chopped basil and remove the pan from the heat.
■ In a bowl, beat the eggs thoroughly. Add the cheese, fold the tomato mixture into the eggs and season well. Replace the pan on the heat, and pour in the remaining oil. Scrape the egg and tomato mixture into the pan, turn the heat down very low and cover. Cook until everything is set, about 20 minutes.
■ Serve at any temperature but chilled.

Cheese and Desserts

Fruit, Cheese and Fruit Salad

FRUTTA, FORMAGGIO E MACEDONIA DI FRUTTA

A word or two in your ear about sweets and the Italian meal. The two do not really go together. When some breathtakingly elegant *antipasto* of, let us say, tiny artichokes eaten whole with lemon juice, oil and black pepper has been consumed, followed by the Stygian perfume of Risotto Nero alle Seppie, a perfect slice of roast veal, its thin, rosemary-scented gravy, and the concentrated summer richness of Melanzane al Forno spicily dressed with chilli and garlic, the discriminating Italian diner is in no mood for Black Forest gateau or apple pie, even if it is written in French. Simple ice cream seems too contrived a choice. No. What the discriminating Italian diner desires is the rude perfection of excellent cheese and the season's fruit at its peak.

Like what? Well? a chunk of fresh, moist Parmesan is always superb. As is Pecorino, either the sweet, *dolce* kind or the hard, spicy one. Fontina and Taleggio are magnificent with firm pears. Dolcelatte and Gorgonzola should be eaten with very fresh Italian bread, on which, with these cheeses, the Italians sometimes scrape a little butter — very unusual. And as for the sight of those huge, lightly-chilled peaches glowing in the bowl at your elbow, it's like that feeling you got in the old days when you knew the insurance would always pay up.

I have given *some* dessert recipes, of course, and I shall begin with the simplest, Macedonia di Frutta, Italian Fruit Salad.

Italian Fruit Salad

MACEDONIA DI FRUTTA

SERVES ABOUT 6
Preparation time 10 minutes
Marinading time at least 4 hours
INGREDIENTS
1¼ cups/300 ml/½ pt fresh orange juice
Zest and juice of one lemon
2 apples
2 firm pears
2 firm bananas
675 g/1½ lb assorted fruit: peaches, apricots, melon, grapes, cherries, mangoes etc
60 ml/4 tbsp white sugar
60 ml/4 tbsp Grappa or Grand Marnier

PREPARATION

■ *Mix the orange juice, lemon juice and zest.*
■ *Peel all the fruit save the grapes and cherries. De-seed everything. As each fruit is peeled, chop it to grape size and add it to the fruit juice mixture immediately to stop it discolouring in the air.*
■ *Sprinkle the sugar over, pour on the liqueur and chill for at least 4 hours if you can. Stir the mixture — carefully — 2 or 3 times during the chilling process.*

Whipped Egg Yolk and Marsala Dessert

ZABAGLIONE

SERVES 6
Preparation time 10–15 minutes
INGREDIENTS
6 eggs
¾ cup/100 g/¼ lb icing (confectioner's) sugar
90 ml/6 tbsp Marsala wine

PREPARATION

■ *Separate the eggs and yolk. Beat the yolks with the sugar and the wine.*

■ *Transfer the bowl containing the egg mixture into the saucepan filled with hot water or pour into the egg mixture into top part of the double-broiler.*

■ *Begin to beat the egg mixture – a fork will not be good enough. Minimum for manual operation is a good, bendy balloon whisk. Ideal is a hand-held electrical version. As the air is incorporated into the eggs, it will swell from the heat of the water. It will also stiffen as the heat of the water cooks it.*

■ *Whisk until the mixture increases its volume by at least 3 times and stiffens until it is only just pourable.*

■ *Decant into fine, fluted glasses. The perfect example would be Venetian in manufacture and Baroque in conception. Eat with spoons and those little biscuits the Italians called amaretti.*

CHEF'S ASIDE

With a very good whisk, this dessert is stunningly simple. The caveat is the usual one with eggs and double-boilers: don't let the water boil and overcook the eggs. You can control the process quite finely by lifting the pan in and out of the water bath.

Here are some unorthodox variations:

■ Add the zest of an orange to the egg mixture before cooking.

■ Add a thumb-sized lump of crystallised ginger – very, very finely sliced.

■ Use port instead of Marsala.

■ Zabaglione can also be a rather classy substitute for cream. With strawberries, for example.

Pick-Me-Up

T I R A M I S U

SERVES 8
Preparation time 2–3 hours

INGREDIENTS

4 eggs

60 ml/4 tbsp Marsala Wine

¾ cup/100 g/¼ lb icing (confectioner's) sugar

225 g/½ lb Mascarpone (or cottage cheese, if stuck)

1¼ cups/300 ml/½ pt strong coffee sweetened with 55 g/2 oz white sugar

40 sponge finger biscuits (about 8 cm/3 in × 2 cm/1 in each)

100 g/¼ lb plain chocolate

PREPARATION

■ Separate the eggs and the yolks. Set aside 2 whites in another bowl.

■ Combine the yolks, the wine and the sugar and beat together.

■ Bring a pan of water to just below boiling, then turn down to simmer and beat the yolk mixture over the water until it begins to swell and thicken. (Use a double boiler or saucepan, if you have one.) Set the yolks aside.

■ Whisk the two remaining whites into stiff peaks and fold them into the yolk mixture, then set aside.

■ Liquidize the cheese in a processor or blender and fold into it the yolk and white mixture. Check the sweetness at this stage and adjust it to taste.

■ Dip each biscuit in the coffee: let it soak well. Arrange a floor of biscuits on your dish then spread the biscuits with a thin coating of the egg/cheese mixture. Repeat the process until you have used your last layer of egg/cheese.

■ Run a knife around the edges of your little building to smooth down the sides. Grate the chocolate and sprinkle it over sides and top. Chill until completely cold and set.

Rice Cake

T O R T A   D I   R I S O

SERVES ABOUT 6
Preparation time 4 hours
Standing time 24 hours
Oven temperature 180° C/ 350° F/Gas 4

INGREDIENTS

4 cups/900 ml/1½ pt milk

Pinch of salt

2 cups/225 g/½ lb white sugar

Zest of 1 lemon

⅓ cup/75 g/3 oz Arborio rice

5 yolks and four whites of eggs

⅓ cup/50 g/2 oz almonds

⅓ cup/50 g/2 oz pine kernels

⅓ cup/50 g/2 oz candied peel

60 ml/4 tbsp Grappa

60 ml/4 tbsp butter, melted

PREPARATION

■ Preheat the oven. Bring milk, salt, sugar and lemon to the boil on top of the stove, and add the rice.

■ Cook until the rice is completely dissolved. The mixture should have the dense consistency of porridge. Remove it from the heat and let it cool.

■ Beat the eggs until well amalgamated.

■ Lightly toast the almonds and pine kernels – but remember, they turn very quickly so do not burn them.

■ Stir the toasted nuts, the candied peel and the Grappa into the rice mixture, then beat it slowly into the eggs.

■ Liberally grease with the butter a cake pan large enough to hold all the mixture. Pour it all in.

■ Bake for about 1 hour, or until the the proverbial knife, proverbially inserted in the centre, comes out as it went in. Let the cake cool until it is easy to handle, but still warm and then ease it from its container.

■ Let it stand, if possible for 24 hours before serving. It will go on improving for a week or so after that.

Ice-Cream

GELATO

SERVES 4
Preparation time about 4 hours maximum
INGREDIENTS
2½ cups/600 ml/1 pt milk
2 vanilla pods
Zest of half a lemon
½ cup/100 g/4 oz white sugar
6 eggs

PREPARATION

■ *Bring the milk to the boil in a saucepan with the vanilla pods, lemon zest and half the sugar. Remove from the heat and let it stand.*

■ *Now separate the egg yolks from the whites and beat the yolks with the sugar.*

■ *Over a double-boiler (see instructions for Zabaglione) beat the egg yolks until they begin to foam and the volume begins to increase. Remove from the heat and slowly beat in the milk.*

■ *Return to the heat and cook slowly for five minutes or so, until you have a liquid the consistency of thick cream. Then, pour the mixture directly into the bowl of your ice-cream machine and switch on, or let the mixture cool to barely lukewarm and freeze. (With the second method, you must beat the mixture well once it has frozen to a slush. This will help to break down the ice crystals, which are an almost inevitable feature of non-paddled ice cream.)*

Conclusion

Italian food is widely misunderstood, a problem for which Italian restaurants outside Italy must share a good deal of the blame. What I have tried to do with the limited number of recipes in this book is to redress the imbalance a little. That is why there are only two dishes involving cream and no recipe for Bolognese sauce. My ability to attempt this feat is thanks principally to two peple: Olga Bernardi of Capanna Kind, a restaurant with rooms near Salice D'Ulzio in the Piedmontese Alps, and her some-time chef Giorgio Raisa from the Veneto, now fortunately both a friend and colleague of mine in England. So cheers to both of you, once again.

I have a feeling, however, that Italian cooking will not remain off the map for long. Things are stirring here, mark my words.

Lastly, the problem of recipes in general. They are compiled with the benefit of hindsight, except in certain cases where some fanatic deliberately tries to create a new dish on paper before cooking it. (It can be done!) It pretty well follows, however, that the recipe is not a tram-line. All it does is describe a sequence of events which happened to a certain extent, by chance. Always remember this. It will free you from the tyranny of cook-books, whose proper place is not in the kitchen but in an armchair by the fireside.

Index

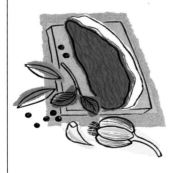